HEART TO HEART
Connection

TOUCHING THE HEART OF GOD:
HIS FAMILY

by
O. Virginia Phillips, Ph.D

"That they all may be one; as Thou, Father art in Me, and I in Thee, that they also may be one in Us; that the world may believe that Thou hast sent me." JOHN 17:21

For information, contact Women of Purpose, Intl.,
P.O. Bo 596, Newberg, OR 97132,
website: www.womenofpurpose.com.
Email: info@womenofpurpose.com

ISBN # 978-0996199216

1. Christian
2. Marriage
3. Family

Published in the Untied States by
Women of Purpose, International
Cover art by Gail Watson

Unless otherwise noted, Scriptures are taken from the Old and
New Testaments in the King James Version of the Bible.

Dedicated to
God's Vineyard,
The Women of Purpose International,
and to my family,
Both biological and extended.

OUR GOD SPEAKS

Be still, and know that I am your God,
I created you when you were but dust and set you apart
In a quiet place to be molded and prepared
For a day and time when My life you would share
To a world in chaos, misery and lost
Not knowing of My sacrifice I paid on the cross
I called and My breath awakened your soul
I spoke and My voice brought knowledge untold
Into your heart awaiting My spirit to unfold

Grace abounding

Faith proclaiming

Love unending

Life enternal

Come unto the arms of I AM and rest.

Taken from "Talking with Jeus" by the author

ACKNOWLEDGMENTS

Some of the information in this book spanned many years of teaching on marriage and the family at churches, conferences and couples meetings in our home. It was not until the year 2000 that I became serious about writing on the Heart to Heart Connection because most of the material I had written in the past was on the family.

I have learned that the relationship God desires begins with a connection to His Heart. If we know what He wants, then we will have a daily infusion of life from His heart to ours. I began to study about the heart and found over a hundred scriptures pertaining to the heart of God.

My late husband, Joshua D. Phillips nudged me on by taking charge of numerous chores around the house to allow me to write, rewrite and even set the manuscript aside while I continued to minister full time. The more I rewrote the more I felt that it would never be completed. It still isn't because there is so much more. I kept adding and subtracting. I have written several manuals on the family, and I borrowed some of the information that I had already written. Finally I eliminated the information because it looked too teacher oriented. When I completed one manuscript, I gave it to two small publishing companies and then asked for it back.

One day Victoria Johnson of Victoria Johnson, Intl, a then board advisor to Women of Purpose, Intl, (the ministry of reconciliation, restoration and renewal that God gave me the vision for in 1993) said "Why don't you write a book? We need a mom for this century." She gave me an assignment to complete the first chapter in one week. After two months of writing and rewriting, I went to the coast for one week and finished five of the seven chapters by writing day and night. It took another 11 months to get it to my good friend and editor, Don Hall.

In this revised edition I give much appreciation to my daughter, Linda Mitchell-Duncan who gave much time retyping and carefully reading all the re-editing done by Mary Lou Knight-Kornbrodt, Administrative Assistant at Women of Purpose, International. I also want to thank Gail Watson, who has worked with the Women of Purpose, International ministry and myself for all these years to use her layout and design skills to make my books and printed material for the ministry look special. She designed the new cover.

I am thankful to my dear friend, Pastor and confidante, David Greenidge, who encourages me personally in ministry and offered Relational Meetings at the Tigard Covenant Church using this book as a guide for Heart to Heart Relationships for marriages, singles, family members and anyone who desires to live a life of abundance in Christ, loving and caring for one another.

To each of you and to Philemon Reid for the original cover design, I am truly grateful.

O. Virginia Phillips

TABLE OF CONTENTS

FOREWORD

This book is more than what the cover implies. It is not a guide for the faint hearted but a passageway to courage, commitment, compassion and strength intended to uplift and inspire all people, believers and nonbelievers. It is a universal cry for the family beginning with the marriage relationship.

This world has its heroes for each decade; this is the decade when the world needs a Mom. Dr. Phillips is that Mom for the 21st Century, for whom we all search for. She is someone who nurtures and loves unconditionally, someone who has proven by her own life that all things are possible when you believe. She is a woman called with a purpose for this time bringing us together in reconciliation, restoration and renewal.

Dr. Phillips (Mom) has an extended family from every culture, ethnic group, religious affiliation and social status. She lives her beliefs, which emanate from God's own Heart.

Victoria Johnson
Victoria Johnson, Intl.

FOREWORD – continued

My husband Bill and I first met Virginia and Joshua Phillips about 22 years ago when we were in the process of adopting a daughter. In our search, we met with the Phillips in their home in Sherwood. Their counsel and support was just what we needed at that time.

We were impressed with the depth and scope of their vision for families then, and we are even more so now. Bill and I were able later on to add a daughter to our family of four sons and, through the 15 years we were involved in Christian publishing, we kept track of Joshua and Virginia and their excellent work with families. And in my ministry to women, Virginia and I have crossed paths several times. Each time we are together, it's like we are best friends again and we have to "catch up!"

I strongly believe that every family - no matter what its size or shape – needs to devour Virginia's book. The times we live in are difficult for families, and we Christians are assaulted by the world as never before. The impact of living in a materialistic, immoral culture touches all of us. Virginia shares in this book a wealth of wisdom and experience that only the test of time and a living walk with God can produce. It is a rare gift to have insight, godly compassion and understanding. Virginia has the unique ability to use her gifts to encourage us to have hope for our families.

Nancie Carmichael
Author; Speaker and former editor of Virtue magazine

PREFACE

There is a flow in the body of Christ that is sweeping through families and churches in such an awe-inspiring way that believers are being caught up in relationships like we have never experienced before. I don't know when I began to recognize its impact. Perhaps it was always there, this seed of love that has grown into an all-encompassing love for people.

As long as I can remember, it has been easy for me to accept people as they are. Perhaps it's because as a child I experienced such a great need to belong. I reach out whenever and wherever I could for a family. I learned early on how to make a family happen, whether it was at the convent school I attended at age 13-1/2, the college I attended at age 18, or with my in-laws, and later with various friends to whom I attached myself. My extended (non-biological) family became a way of life for me.

Extended family was also a way of life for my mother. Before I was born, she had given shelter to several distant cousins and friends who needed a family for a time. Later when I had my own family we took our first foster child into our home when my eighth child, Kenneth, was less than a year old. At the time, it was against the rules of the state child welfare agency in California, but Yvonne was the only African American girl at the Los Guilucos Home for Girls at that time, and she needed a family to visit on weekends. Before we could make a final decision the worker brought her to our home. She moved in after two visits. She lived with us for 1-1/2 years before returning to San Bernardino to live with her biological mother. That was only the beginning. Our home became a refuge for displaced children. My heart became a sanctuary for any child in need.

After my first husband, Roy Mitchell, died suddenly at 38 of an embolism in 1974, I lived for 4-1/2 years as a widow raising eight children on my own. We had a $10,000 life insurance policy and owed $8,000 in bills, so that first year, I learned to depend upon God for everything. During that time, as the scripture says, God became my husband, friend and confidante. We had a close relationship. Each month all our expenses were met and my faith was more than belief. It was a gift. Perhaps it was during this time that I began to understand how near my heart was to God. I certainly began to know Him for myself – not only as someone to pray to and trust, but someone to listen to and understand.

During this time, Joel 2:12 was so real.

"Therefore also now, saith the Lord, turn ye even to me with all your heart, and with fasting, and with weeping, and with mourning: ..."

Our fellowship was not broken but my heart was and God did bind up and heal my broken heart as promised in Isaiah 61:1.

My professional friends would send their children to live with me during the summers not realizing that I could have used help myself. It worked only because my children helped and welcomed the other children into our home. When we moved to Oregon from California in 1975, my family's home again became a haven for hurting children. Sometimes I felt that there must have been a sign outside my door not visible to me but clear to others: "If you need a mother, I'm available."

The principles in this book evolved as I connected to the heart of God in my marriage relationship with my first husband. When Roy died I learned from that season of my life to totally depend upon Jesus in order to become bonded in a loving relationship that provided me with the friendship I longed for. Only God could provide the commitment I sought and the communication I needed when there was no one else to confide in. When God brought

Joshua, my second husband, into my life, I had finally learned to apply the principles of a happy family to my home. The education I received through life's lessons, some of which are related in this book, could have been tragic. Instead these lessons were preparation for a mature marriage and family. Each lesson connected me closer to God's heart.

As I thought about the different lessons which became crossroads in this Heart to Heart Connection, I remembered a narrative that I read by my friend LaDean Caducoy, a missionary and former prayer coordinator for Women of Purpose International. She wrote "Heart's Journey" and she permitted it to be printed here. It is printed on the following page.

You created me, to love, so give me the wisdom
to follow all your commands.

"May all who fear you find in me
a cause for joy,
for I have put my hope
in your word."

Psalm 119:74 (NLT)

HEART'S JOURNEY

I looked and saw a heart
Heart was wounded and bleeding
Jesus came to Heart and touched him
giving heart home and promise.
Heart looked and saw the promise
Filled with hope
Heart began to walk toward the promise
Oh, the journey was so difficult,
with many hindrances.
But Heart was determined to press on to the promise.
After some time, Jesus came to Heart
stopping Heart in his path.
"Heart, look at the promise" Jesus said.
Heart looked, then gasped
The promise has become more distant on the horizon!"
Panicked, Heart began to run forward
Jesus stopped Heart again and said
"Heart, look behind you"
"Oh no!" exclaimed Heart,
I cannot do that
The pain from my wound is too great
I must continue toward the promise
I must show You my love by fulfilling
the promise You gave me."
Heart began to proceed
but Jesus gently put his hands on Heart's shoulders
Looking into Heart's eyes, Jesus said
"If you love Me, you will obey Me"
As Jesus turned Heart around, he said
"Now look and see what I have to show you"

Heart looked…and saw a jagged trail of blood
which came to Heart's feet.
Heart wailed, "See Jesus
this wound of mine is bleeding!
I don't like to look at it
The promise is much more beautiful."
Jesus said, "Heart, look closer."
As heart looked again, he saw the trail of blood
was really many other wounded, bleeding hearts.
Stunned, Heart dropped to his knees
Jesus gently said
"Humble yourself and I will lift you up"
Tears flowed freely down Heart's face as he cried
"My Lord, I repent! I repent!"
Heart was compelled to move backward
as he knelt before Jesus.
Heart's tears fell upon the wounded, each and everyone
When Heart came to the place where the trail had once begun,
Heart's tears subsided and dried
A sense of righteousness and purity washed over Heart
Jesus, still standing before Heart
bent to offer His hand to Heart and said
"Arise and see"
With Jesus' help, Heart stood and looked to find
the jagged, bloody trail was completely gone!
With a smile, Jesus spoke, "Now see the promise."
Heart looked up and was astonished to see
the promise was nowhere on the horizon!
Alarmed and bewildered, Heart looked to Jesus
who was still smiling at Heart.

Jesus answered the question in Heart's eyes by
a simple gesture with His hand toward Heart's own heart
and Heart's eyes followed
To Heart's amazement, the old wound
was nowhere to be found!
More wondrous, Heart saw he had become
transparent and now could see
the beautiful promise was within him
Inquiringly, Heart looked to Jesus
Jesus responded, "The promise is exactly
where I put it when I gave it to you"
"But…" stammered Heart
"I saw the promise on the horizon"
"The wound clouded your vision and distorted
your understanding" Jesus answered
Then Jesus took Heart's hand and said
"Come now, fulfill my joy by living in harmony,
being of the same mind, and one in purpose,
having the same love
Do nothing from strife, selfishness or for unworthy ends
prompted by conceit and arrogance
Instead, in the true spirit of humility let
each regard the other as better than himself."
So, hand in hand
Jesus and Heart joyfully journeyed together

LaDean Caducoy

The heart is a sanctuary where God dwells. His Spirit flows through each chamber, filling it with His Spirit. Out of these rooms flow perfect Love, Joy, Peace, Long-suffering, Endurance and Hope. Is it any wonder that there is a longing for a heart connect to the Creator of such perfection?

O. Virginia Phillips

INTRODUCTION

Proverbs 4:23 tells us,

"Keep thy heart with all diligence; for out of it are the issues of life."

The human heart is a life-giving pump, a simple machine with a sacred mission. Its fabric is coarse, yet the heart connects and sustains the body's work. Cardiac rhythm allows the brain to think, the lungs to breathe and the muscles to move.

The ancient physicians saw the heart as a mystery, but all supported the fact that the heart is the root of life. Aristotle said, "Nature does nothing without a purpose." He maintained that in the hearts moist warmth could be found the "seat of the senses and the domain of the soul. There, pulsed the soul's vital spirit which contracts and expands naturally and so is able to pace and to thrust from one and the same cause." He believed that the brain, consisting of water and earth, serves as a radiator to cool hot blood from the heart.

In the 1600s, Miguel Servetus, a Spanish theologian and physician, maintained, "He who really understands what is involved in the breathing of man has already sensed the breath of God." Through the study of anatomy, Servetus sought a rational explanation for the Biblical passage placing man's soul in the blood. He wondered how the breath of God reached the blood. Servetus' work, published in 1553, described the path of blood from the heart to the lungs. He had discovered pulmonary circulation. In doing so, he challenged the wisdom of Galen, the 2nd Century Greek physician, whose doctrines had survived to the Middle Ages to become dogma.[1]

Servetus noted that blood traveled from the right side of the

---

[1]Davis, Good P., *The Heart: The Living Pump*, Forstar Books, 1981

heart to the other side by way of a "lengthened passage through the lungs, which the blood is elaborated and becomes a crimson color." After mixing with the air in the lungs, the blood became "a fit dwelling place for the vital spirit" and finally entered the left ventricle of the heart. Blood circulates in a state of ceaseless movement driven by the heart's pumping action. Servetus describes the arteries as "vessels carrying blood from the heart to the body, the veins returning blood from the body to the heart."

Thereafter, studies of the heart produced modern diagnostic tools that have given the heart a thousand faces. Its anatomy became artistry through x-rays, computers and video equipment. Physicians study bold, revealing likenesses of the human heart, seeing its beauty and vulnerability in stark detail.

Yet, with all this massive knowledge, there is still a part of the heart, the part connected to God's heart that is hidden to man. And that is the incorruptible heart, barely touch by the physician, but acknowledged, nevertheless, by the ancients who proclaimed in agreement that the heart is the center of life; a creative masterpiece.

From the heart of God springs life, bound to the virtues of honor, love and courage. The heart ties body to spirit, the mystical past to the practical present.

Who can know the heart except its Creator? Jeremiah 17:10 states, **"I the Lord search the heart, I try the reins, ..."** My prayer for myself and for all who read this book is that God will strengthen our hearts and the hearts of our families so that we will all know Him, love Him and obey Him.

God gives us a heart connection so that eternal life will flow from His heart to ours. Let our prayer be as the prayer of Jesus to the Father, in John 17:21.

> **"That they all may be one; as thou, Father, art in me, and I in thee, that they also may be one in us: ..."**

This book is written with three goals in mind. The first, is to minister to families, both biological and extended, beginning with the relationship between husband and wife. The second, is how relationships are connected beginning with the experience of belonging and ending with the Love connection which is the completion of a Heart to Heart relationship and the third, is to answer the question of whether a social service system created to protect and help children can become an agent for keeping families together.

To belong is a bonding experience; an
experience that opens the heart to relationships
with others in an ebb and flow
that refreshes the soul
like a stream on parched soil.
It is an answer to a desperate
need for love.

O. Virginia Phillips
Romans 8:35

1

THE BELONGING CONNECTION
JOY

Growing up, from the ages 5 to 12, I was my mother's helper. I belonged to her. Even through the painful times of hard work and loneliness, there was something that kept me focused. During my elementary years my mother tried to show me how much she loved me by taking me with her when she traveled.

At age 7, she took me to Cleveland, Ohio, to meet my father. She thought that this would be a way of giving me a better chance at life. It didn't work. I felt no connection to my father. He was not present in my early years and by age 7, I already had a stepfather. My natural father was a stranger.

At age 13, my mother left me with distant cousins in Milwaukee, Wisconsin whom I had not met until then. It was her way of giving me a better chance to succeed in life, something that she felt she could not do. I remember longing for a family at that transitional age because I had so many questions.

Later I came to the realization that my mother's love was deeper than I could have understood at age 13. Although it might have appeared that she abandoned me, I knew that in her own way, she was trying to introduce me to a better life. She did it the only way she knew how. She had taught me to work at an early age and encourage my curiosity and dreams that were bigger than life. She told me that she knew I could 'make it" because I had faith in God and the courage to believe for more than she could ever give me. Mother prayed therefore God undoubtedly guided her in a way that most could not understand.

Age 13 is a very vulnerable age. I know now that it was part of the destiny that God had planned for me. My objective was education and somehow I knew I could make something of myself. All the time it was God molding me.

Before my mother left to return to Arkansas to take care of my two younger sisters, she and I lived in an upstairs flat, which we shared with two married couples. The rent was split three ways, but when my mother left, I had to pay a third of the rent on my own. And although my room was the smallest in the flat and my cousin put his mother in my room, the amount of rent remained the same.

To earn money, I exaggerated my real age so I could work. I was hired to help dress the models at an exclusive dress Shoppe called Metz's in downtown Milwaukee, Wisconsin.

My mother's prayers, her internal and external impartation of courage and work ethic, my insatiable desire for an education, along with God's grace, led me to St. Benedict the Moor Catholic boarding school. I was the only boarder without a family at this school for upper-middle class girls and I had to work to pay my way through high school. During this time, the nuns and priests became my family. The Mother Superior and Sister Albina became my surrogate mothers.

At age 18, I went to another all-girls school, a college where I was the only African-American on the campus. I obtained a scholarship to attend the Cardinal Stritch College for women (now located in Brown Deer, Wisconsin). I worked hard to get that scholarship because there was no other way for me to get a college education.

I was hundreds of miles away from my mother. I had few friends because my time had been spent working my way through high school. There was little time to connect with friends except for one or two...maybe. My heart ached for friendship. I needed someone to talk with, to share my pain and understand my feelings. I would bury my head into my pillow at night, screaming inside, but only soft moaning traveled from my broken heart to my lips as I squeezed my eyes shut to abate the tears. "Why don't I have a roommate? I asked myself. But I knew why. No one knew me so no one signed up to share my space. I was not antisocial, I was a friendly person. A little shy sometimes, but open to meeting new people. In fact, I remember wishing that college would be different from high school where I had spent most of my time studying and working and little time with my friends.

On a cold November night, I began to think about the events in my life that had brought me to where I was. I felt alone and rejected. I remembered a phrase from my mother that molded my resolve to live and make something of myself: "Ofidean, I wanted you." Ofidean is the name my mother and grandmother made up. It means faith. I sign my name O. Virginia. In the Catholic Church, I needed a Christian name and "Ofidean" didn't fit, so Virginia was added. "Ofidean" became my connection to my faith identity, which I held dear to my heart.

I didn't understand how important that sentence ("Ofidean, I wanted you.") was to the ebb and flow of my life, but at age 19, it was my emotional anchor. I belonged to someone – to my mother and God – who wanted me. For the moment, the loneliness and rejection dissipated as I dreamed of how things would turn out. My Belonging Connection enabled me to dream myself out of what could have been a time of great depression.

Since that time, the seasons of my life have shown me the process of how life connects the heart from one person to another because of what happens in the beginning of one's growth and development. The very process of bonding can only come if a planted seed has, as its connection, a belonging principle. A person can withstand any hardship if she or he "belongs" to someone who loves her or him. To belong is to be accepted in the heart of another. It is a life flow that establishes the foundation for success or failure.

I have watched children who have a belonging connection to someone but have very little food, hardly any clothes and live in shacks. Yet they prosper in relationships with others because their life began with someone they belonged to and who accepted them.

I remember a particular child that my second husband, Joshua, spoke of frequently as we watched numerous disconnected children dealing with depression, loneliness and rejection.

During the 1960s and '70s, Joshua was director and chaplain at a correctional institution in Ohio. One of the young boys in his cottage was forbidden by his social worker to return home due to the poor, unsightly condition of the house and the lack of a designated caregiver, there were several cousins and uncles in the three-room house. Some were alcoholics. Often times, there was little food to feed the many who resided in the house. The foundation of the house was eroding, the blankets that hung as window curtains had holes in them and the front door was held together with two pieces of plywood and some nails. To the social worker's eye, the place was unfit for anyone to live in, especially a 12-year old child. Aaron (not his real name) had been placed in the institution at age 10 for stealing food for his family. It was something he had done consistently until authorities followed him to this house and took him away. Aaron was depressed the entire time he was in the institution. The social worker sent him to a psychologist, but to no avail. It was believed that his depression stemmed from poor upbringing and not having proper clothes, food, housing and nurturing.

Joshua felt differently about the boy's situation because the only time Aaron smiled was when he spoke of his family. He would refuse to eat and would curse at the social workers, who would

4

eventually punish him by leaving him alone in his room. Joshua noticed that Aaron was very belligerent and acted out, usually around the holidays. On the second thanksgiving that Aaron was in the institution, he begged Joshua to take him home for a visit. Joshua convinced the social worker to allow the visit, promising to remain with Aaron the entire time and to bring him back to the institution the same day. The director of the institution, the social worker and the psychological team reluctantly agreed.

Joshua drove Aaron to the country shack outside of Cleveland. About three miles from the house, Aaron's countenance changed. He began to talk excitedly about his relatives, especially his Uncle George. According to Aaron, his uncle had been a war hero who, after returning home couldn't find a job. He spent most of his time, especially during the summers, fishing. During the winter, he would hunt a little and then disappear. However, Aaron could remember, from age 3 on up, how his Uncle George would spend time with him. He would tell him, "No matter how poor you are, remember you have someone who loves you." Aaron belonged to someone. His heart connected to his Uncle George.

When Aaron arrived at his house he jumped out of the car before it could stop completely and ran up to the makeshift door. For the first time, Joshua actually heard Aaron laugh out loud. The boy was transformed in an instant. He was greeted by a myriad of adults welcoming him home. As his eyes darted to and fro, they finally fell upon the person he longed for, his Uncle George. Joshua found out later that Uncle George only returned on Thanksgiving and Christmas, always hoping to see Aaron.

Joshua walked in and introduced himself to Uncle George. No one else seemed to care whether he was there or not. No one cared that the air was blowing through the blankets in the window or that the door did not close all the way. Aaron was home and Uncle George was hugging the only person he really cared about. Aaron connected with this reality – he belonged.

Joshua and Aaron left several hours later and they returned to the institution, with the understanding that Joshua would take Aaron to visit his Uncle George during the Christmas season. After the Thanksgiving visit, Aaron opened his heart to Joshua who became his friend and father image. Aaron allowed himself to connect to Joshua, opening him up to other bonds of friendship. He left the institution at age 18, having completed high school. Joshua encouraged him to complete his education and go on to graduate school. Aaron returned from teaching junior high school and has his own family. His ability to succeed came from his early connection with a family member. That connection allowed him to bond with Joshua and eventually others.

Belonging, synonymous with acceptance, prepares the heart to receive others. In fact, a child that does not bond to at least one person at an early age is susceptible to relational failures. Relational failure is similar to heart failure. When there is an emotional and spiritual blockage, the arteries of communication – friendship, commitment and submission – cease to flow.

The book of Proverbs counsels, "*A merry heart maketh a cheerful countenance, but by sorrow of the heart the spirit is broken.*" Hearts not only break, they sing, cry, melt or turn hard as stone, become light or heavy, warm or cold. All depending on the heart connection or lack of connection to another. When belonging and bonding occur a supportive foundation is provided enabling a relationship to build.

The heart circulates the blood. It is durable, yet delicate and sustains the body's 60,000-mile cardiovascular system with and 11-ounce pump. By the heart's power, man lives. The heart, in its physiological creation has a mission. It is the center of life. William Harvey, a 17th century physician, deemed the heart "the sovereign of the body." A similar occurrence happens in relationships. Just as the heart sustains the flow of life blood the body, relationships sustain life emotionally and spiritually so that man can wholly connect to the vast purpose of his creation and to his Creator.

6

To belong is to connect with God and to other human beings in a relationship that provides a bridge to spiritual and emotional health. Relationships, like the physical heart, kindle and keep spiritual and emotional life ablaze. Physical, spiritual and emotional relationships create a belonging connection producing life. When fitly joined, every joint supplies what the total body needs. The heart ties the body to the spirit and the first principle that guides a heart-connected family comes from belonging. Belonging creates a bond that cannot be broken. (Ephesians 4:16)

"From him the whole body, joined and held together by every supporting ligament, grows and builds itself up in love, as each part does its work."

Bonding occurs in many ways and at specific times in one's life. It begins in the mother's womb where a child experiences every heartbeat of the mother. In the first trimester of growth, the child hears, smells and senses pain. This is a time when the child can hear the voice of the father and mother, a time when internal bonding begins.

Bonding continues throughout pregnancy when the preparation and cultivation of the soil for good relationships between parent and the child begins. Internal bonding is an impartation of one's spirit that can affect the attitude and personality of a child. When parents take time to pray for a child nestled just below the heart of the mother, when they sing songs and speak peace into the child's spirit and lay hands on the mother's stomach, there is a definite bonding that occurs inside the womb.

External bonding begins at birth, as the child is laid upon the mother's breast and the father holds the child next to his heart. These bonding times should be stressed more by physicians and hospital caregivers but especially by parents. It makes a great difference in how relationships begin in a child's life.

Babies who are not touched by parents in the early stages of the baby's development lack nurturing attachments. In some U.S. hospitals, mothers and grandparents are encouraged to volunteer to hold babies. The need for touching and nurturing, especially near the heart, is essential for healthy bonding. If this is left out of a child's life in the early stages, it creates a void and as the child grows, he or she has difficulty trusting.

Long before I began to study the effect of internal and external bonding, I understood it from my mother. Although I don't remember spending a lot of time with my mother because she worked outside of the home, I do remember her saying that I was wanted even before conception. An internal seed from my mother's thoughts was planted in me the entire nine months that she carried me. There was an expectancy that my mother imparted to me. In fact, she specifically asked God for a girl, that I would be special and that I would love to read. She spoke into my life before I was born and I became all that she asked for. I was the only child in the family that she prayed for in this way. I never understood why, but I knew that I was different from the rest of my siblings. In fact, except for my relationship with my mother, most of my relationships were with people outside of my birth family.

Belonging happens when there is a spiritual and natural heart connection. The psalmist David was a man after God's own heart, not because he was a perfect man, but because he had a relationship with God. When there is a relational life flow between two or more persons the spiritual heart connection is an impartation that flows from the heart of God and connects His people together in a bond of love.

BONDING: In marriage is a unting force or tie. It is a binding agreement, a union or cohesion between partners.

"Therefore shall a man leave his father and mother, and shall cleave unto his wife: and they shall be one flesh." (Genesis 2:24)

Many marriages end in divorce because this bonding between the husband and wife never occurs. When a man leaves his mother and father and cleaves to his wife a relationship begins which should establish a priority between a couple that no one else can alter. A cementing takes place and the two entities are fused into one.

This is the reason God judges fornication and adultery so harshly. He even went so far as to say that whosoever joins his body to a harlot becomes one flesh with that harlot. If a married man makes his bed with a harlot, he has sinned against God, his own body and that of his wife because his body belongs to Christ and he and his wife are one flesh. His body through marriage is no longer his alone but also hers (I Corinthians 6:15-16).

Bonding takes place when each partner develops sensitivity toward the other's needs. This sensitivity occurs as our minds are transformed, so that we can prove what the will of God is (Romans 12:2). Sensitivity to our mates comes through taking quality time to listen and being willing to bear each other's burdens. (Galations 6:2)

"Bear ye one another's burdens, and so fulfil the law of Christ."

Everyone has a blind side, but instead of exposing the blind side, marriage partners should edify and build on each other's strengths and pray for their weaknesses until the person is strong enough to work at changing them. As the word of God tells us, we who are strong ought to bear the weaknesses of those without strength and not just please ourselves (Romans 15:1). Jesus is the model in the bonding process, for even Christ did not please Himself but God. It is written:

"...The reproaches of them that reproached thee fell on me." (Romans 15:3)

There has to be an understanding in a marriage that deferring to one another's needs will not hamper the relationship but enhance it. Bonding happens through nurturing, listening, time away from routine, deferring to the other, accepting one another's needs as our own, showing mercy in a weakness and, above all, remembering that whatever affects one affects the other.

There is a method used in marriage counseling called "transference", where one member of a marriage union is asked to take the place of the other in a troubling situation. This is done in the interest of strengthening the marriage.

"Transference" occurs in a Christian marriage when one partner prays and asks God to allow him or her to feel what the other person is feeling in order to understand the needs of the other and become sensitive to the emotions and expectations of the other. This method is used with couples who have come to an impasse in their relationship. It is a process of communication, touching and listening to develop sensitivity toward the other person.

Bonding takes place over a period of time. Bonding between a married couple is like a baby bonding to its mother. Through nurturing the baby gets to know the mother's touch, really sees the mother and focuses attention toward her, and the baby has its needs met unconditionally.

A baby has only himself to give. Often the mother does not love the child deeply at first, until they spend time together. The child's personality begins to develop, the demand on a mother's time diminishes, and the child begins to obey some of the mother's wishes. This bonding is important to the furtherance of the parent-child relationship. Expectations increase on the part of the mother as the child begins to understand what the mother expects. A similar relationship occurs in marriage.

In the Old Testament (Deuteronomy 24:5), when a man took a wife he was told he should not go to war or be charged with any duty. He should be free at home for one year and to give happiness to his new wife.

In the first year of marriage, couples should spend time getting to know one another, sensing needs, being together and developing a strong sensitive relationship. This seldom happens in our society, so it is no wonder that divorce is so widespread! Many couples that have been married 20 to 30 years suddenly find themselves getting divorced for numerous reasons, but they cannot explain how it all began. This often happens when bonding does not take place in the early years of marriage.

Married couples should understand that they are the priority. Even children should not interfere with their relationship to each other. New mothers should be wise and organize their time in such a way that the husband's time with her is not usurped. Children learn by example. If precious loving time is spent together, children will learn to relate this to their own lives later. Teach your children about marriage early through "modeling."

MODELING: Demonstrating through one's lifestyle the attributes needed to teach good character and strong relationship in a marriage.

Too often women complain about their husband's lack of affection and understanding. Usually, in such cases, the husband's father did not demonstrate these attributes. Women shouldn't wait for a man to teach their sons about the emotional needs of a woman especially if the husband is not the way she wants him to be. Women can be and should be instructors of their children.

They can teach their sons about women. Even if the father is not openly demonstrative, a woman can be. Non-demonstrative men often marry women who are demonstrative. A woman should be sensitive to this side of her husband, understanding that she is the part that he isn't and together they make up a whole person. Even if bonding does not occur in the first year, couples can concentrate on their marriage bond throughout their married life and rekindle their love periodically.

CLEAVING: **Joining together in one flesh and one spirit, in a covenant relationship that cannot be broken.**

Cleaving takes place in the process of building a relationship. Couples are to be of one mind in their compassion for one another. Though they are married, they are also sister and brother in Christ. And the same expectation that God has for the church family applies to married couples (I Peter 3:8).

Cleaving also takes place when spouses refrain from speaking evil of one another and treat one another as their first human priority. We will see in the chapter on communication that the words we speak to each other can bring togetherness or divorce. It is important that, as married people, we remember to pursue peace in our marriage relationship through the process of building and bonding and seeking to do good to one another as unto the Lord.

A husband or wife should not tear down the relationship but build it up as we are told to build the church through edification and encouragement. In the bonding process, husbands are to dwell with their wives according to knowledge (they are to know them), giving the wife honor because they are heirs together in God's kingdom. Speaking disrespectfully and belittling the wife will cause the husband's prayers to be hindered (I Peter 3:7). This then can bring about depression, bitterness and resentment. Wives also are to honor their husbands.

When Joshua and I married both of us were widowed. He was 13 years my senior. I needed a godly man with great wisdom because I had been alone with my eight children for almost five years. Our first year of marriage was spent listening. We talked for hours about our expectations, our feelings about children, ministry, and our social and personal lives. We left no subject that was important to us unspoken.

Spending time together was so important to us that we would rise up early to pray together. After the children were off to school, we spent most the day communicating. Joshua did not work the first year and neither did I. He spent his retirement money to care for the home because our relationship was so important. We went into ministry to families and children as a team because we listened to each other and to God.

BONDING REQUIRES THREE THINGS:

BONDING REQUIRES <u>PREPARATION</u>: A family that practices the belonging connection will be a healthy family. It begins even before the marriage vows are spoken. Couples who are planning their marriage should come into an agreement about how their children are to be reared. They should discuss the number of children they plan to have and how they will discipline them.

Character building should be part of the premarital discussion and counseling too. After marriage and parenthood, the father should practice blessing his children and both should pray into the lives of their unborn while the child is in the womb. The fruit of the spirit should be prayed into the child's life daily – love, joy, peace, patience, kindness, goodness, faithfulness, gentleness and self-control.

One scripture that bears witness to the impartation in the womb is Luke 1:41:

> *"And it came to pass, that, when Elisabeth heard the salutation of Mary, that the babe leaped in her womb; and Elisabeth was filled with the Holy Ghost."*

In our family seminars, the question is often asked, "If bonding does not occur in the womb or early in the child's life, what chance is there of bonding occurring later?" There is always a need in a child or adult to bond to someone. Bonding that occurs after age 8 will take longer because relational misconceptions, hurts, neglect and rejection result from early lack of bonding. It takes intervention from God to heal this failure of a heart connection. Many examples in scripture illustrate God's mercy in very hard cases of such woundedness. On classic example is the woman at the well (John 4). We don't know that she didn't bond at childhood, but her actions in adulthood suggest that she had poor relational skills. She had married five times and the man she was with when she met Jesus was not her husband, but her life changed when she met the Savior.

A belonging connection does not guarantee freedom from adversity – it prepares us for it. Adversity happens in the lives of God's people for a purpose. The Holy Spirit searches the hearts of man and knows the mind of God. When rejection comes God can turn it into His own purpose and plan.

Romans 8:28-29:

"And we know that all things work together for good to them that love God, to them who are the called according to his purpose. For whom he did foreknow, he also did predestinate to be conformed to the image of his Son, that he might be the firstborn among many brethren."

BONDING REQUIRES <u>TIME</u>: Spending time together is very important. It begins with the father and mother. Two people who plan to spend the rest of their lives together need time to share precious moments together. Couples should have time alone weekly without interference from anyone. Families need to appreciate their time together more than any other relationships. Weekly family meetings (explained in detail in the communication chapter) are a must for today's families. Their togetherness can be put in a special memory book for the next generation.

BONDING REQUIRES <u>LOVE</u>: Love is the glue that holds a family together. It is absolutely necessary for the family that learns to endure all things. When parents divorce one another the children are also divorced to the degree that the wholeness of a unit is separated into different parts.

When a man and woman marry they are no longer two but one. Like two pieces of paper that were once glued together, in order to separate them a tearing occurs. The papers are marred and they are no longer the same. This happens in a divorce. The foundation that was originally bonded – father, mother and children – is torn apart. Marriage is a covenant between God and two people. When a marriage covenant is broken we must remember that Jesus is our mediator. We must make our confession and repentance to Him as well as our spouse and children. A broken covenant is a sin and it must be forgiven.

Hebrew 12:24:

"And to Jesus the mediator of the new covenant, and to the blood of sprinkling, that speaketh better things than that of Abel."

Bonding brings unity to a family. Bonding allows each person to be accepted in his or her diversity. Children in the same family have different personality traits, although they look alike on the outside. For example, my sisters and I have the same mother but we are totally different.

At the age of 7, I took care of my younger sisters, ages 5 and 3. They remained in Arkansas when my mother first took me to Ohio. While I was between the ages of 8 and 11, we were a unit. Even though I wanted to play outside, I knew my mother needed me to keep the house clean and watch my sisters while she worked. I washed and ironed clothes at the age of 8. I wanted to help my mother because it pleased her and she taught me to be dependable.

Working at such a young age was not an issue. It was the bond that held our family together that was important. In a family, each member should endeavor to keep unity, which comes from the spirit of God and bonds them together in peace (Ephesians 4:3).

In my counseling practice, I am often asked: Can a foster child bond when moved from home to home? Consider this real episode of a young girl who lived in foster care but never bonded because she wanted her own family.

"I want to go home to my Mom. I don't like being in foster care and I want to visit my own relatives. I have some cousins around the corner from here I can visit. My uncle wants me to come to his house for Thanksgiving dinner." —Dezzie W.

All day Wednesday—the day before Thanksgiving—Dezzie, an African American child, talked about her family, her dozens of extended biological family members in Louisiana and California. But just before the important day when families traditionally get together and give thanks for a myriad of blessings, Dezzie was with people she barely knew.

Dezzie's mother is a victim of cocaine abuse and she had lost all five of her children to the state. If she knew how to work with the system, she could have probably seen her children on a consistent basis. But too often she got depressed and fearful and she still used cocaine. Dezzie's mother could not save herself from destruction; she was in denial and dealing with her guilt and the state could not help her. The mother needed a special kind of support system. Even if she had gone into a professionally operated rehabilitation program, she would still be vulnerable to drugs. The root of her problem was not her abuse of drugs but a lack of life management skills, which cover a plethora of dysfunctions.

There are too many Americans like Dezzie's mother. The welfare system could offer Dezzie substitute care, but cannot give Dezzie what she really wanted and needed, her mother. The state spent thousands of dollars yearly to keep Dezzie in a system that failed to give her what she needed and will eventually spend more to keep Dezzie's siblings.

16

Foster care was not the long-term solution to Dezzie's problems. She was only provided custodial care if she remained there, because she won't or cannot bond to temporary custodians. Too many children like Dezzie don't bond and they take to the streets, become runaways and their lives are wasted.

Dezzie left her foster home. The pressure of not being with her brothers and sisters was too much, so she walked away from the foster home to a relative's house. Since her social worker didn't know all of Dezzie's relatives (their names were not given to the foster parents), the foster parents' only recourse was to call 911.

If the police happened to pick Dezzie up, she would have spent Thanksgiving in a juvenile detention home when all she really wanted to do was go home for Thanksgiving. The fact that her mother used drugs is of no consequence to Dezzie; it was her mother and they belonged together. There were other members of the family that did not use drugs, but they could not house Dezzie because of the additional cost. In some states, the child welfare system does not pay relatives to keep children within the family.

This brings us back to a basic common sense question: What is the best situation for Dezzie—her family or foster care? Let's explore this situation further.

Dezzie didn't function well in foster care, nor did she function in school. Her mind was constantly on her brothers and sisters. Teachers could not force her to remain in class because they were not allowed to touch her. Dezzie said she could do anything she wanted to do because the teachers could not do anything to her, and Dezzie had not learned self-discipline.

The problem was that Dezzie wanted her own family and she could not have them. Without constant supervision (this was her third foster care placement within a year), Dezzie will continue to walk out because she cannot bond to her foster family. What is the solution? Let's explore the following possibilities.

Good family planning could bring a solution to Dezzie's problem. The priority of any child welfare system should be to strengthen the family unit. Dezzie's mother is not abusive to her. Her mother was a victim of her own emotional dysfunction. If the parent is abusive, another plan of action must be taken, but in this case, a parent support group could be made available, consisting of individuals who have successfully "kicked the habit" and those who are willing to talk and encourage Dezzie's mother on a daily basis.

Part of the mother's problem is that when she decides to kick her drug habit, the only friends she has will still be taking drugs. Kicking a drug habit is not something a person can do in isolation. Dezzie's mother needed a non-biological extended family that would help her until she could stand steadfast and recognize who she can be. She needed reality therapy in a support group with others who understand her issues, who will not reject her and can be there for her.

Such a support system might be needed for one or even two years. It's worth the time and expense because it could provide consistency and self-discipline to Dezzie's mother and eventually allow Dezzie and her siblings to return home. It would also save the state money in the long run because the system will eventually no longer need to support Dezzie's family.

A support services network for Dezzie's mother and her siblings would include:

• Family support facilitators for substance abuse parents to meet on a weekly basis. This support group should be based in the local community. Dezzie's mother is an African-American. The facilitators should understand the survivalist mentality of African-Americans and their cultural need for extended family support.

• Community recovery programs where parents can go to receive the professional help they need.

• Extended families (physical or spiritual) who allow parents to visit with their children until the parent has recovered from substance abuse.

In a support system of this type, the child is not completely removed from family members. The parent and child visit each other at the recommendation of the parent support group facilitator. Visits can be made in the extended family home or the support group facility. If it is the support group facility, it should be homey, comfortable and conducive to family visitation without pressure.

A community process like this would enable the strengthening of families without the permanent separation of children from their natural families. Too often, the child welfare system's first plan is to separate the child from the biological family, which can eventually destroy the child, and the family may never regain the ability to reunite.

In small towns, the problem is somewhat different from larger metropolitan areas. Foster parents often know the child's family, and family members are sometimes only blocks from the foster parents. When the caseworker tries to restrict family visitations, it doesn't work. It should be ok for Dezzie to go home on holidays. She would not have to run away if the plan were implemented to meet her emotional needs and that of her mother. Over time, such a plan would cost the state less, strengthen the family and revitalize high-risk families.

I believe that an extended family system with a continuum of child-oriented programs can be established. After all, nurtured children usually produce nurturing adults. The child welfare system reflects a gross lack of understanding of the different needs of children who are born into different family cultures and traditions.

FAMILY PRESERVATION MODEL:

"Family preservation" is a movement to return a child to the original family whenever possible. The fact is the children welfare system in the 21st Century, is equipped with limited child rearing models and one method of child rearing will not accommodate the needs of all the children. We need to respect different approaches to child rearing. The extended family system recommends caring for the endangered child by whoever is best qualified in the child's own biological family, culture and neighborhood.

Before a family is provided Family Preservation support, there needs to be an assessment of the family unit that involves the entire family – whether led by a single parent or a couple. What do the parents want for their children? Ask the question. Do they really want the child or children? If they don't, they should not be forced to keep them and eventually their children.

A neighborhood support advocate who knows the family and has a desire to help should be provided. The advocate should be trained with the skills needed to support the children while the parents are given options. There should be a simultaneous search for support persons – biological relatives or church members – that the children know. As part of the Family Preservation process, a component should be in place to train willing neighborhood families to keep children in the family neighborhood, if the child feels safe with such neighbors and in that neighborhood.

In African American communities, often a church person is willing to keep an endangered child but caregivers need basic support (food and clothing allowances) and medical support. Because the welfare system has been so punitive toward relatives of children in the welfare system, it will take time and consistent input from culturally different communities to bring about desired results. It will cost less in the long run and children will be better cared for overall.

SPIRITUAL PARENTING MODEL:

The ideal for children who have relatives who do not love them enough to provide a safe and caring home is to give such children an opportunity to bond with people who have a heart connect to God. The church has been given that responsibility. Displaced children are just as orphaned as those without living parents. We are to bring the poor who are cast out into our homes.

In 1986, Joshua and I moved from our comfortable family home in Sherwood, Oregon to Portland in response to a need by the state children's division for a group home for displaced girls. Extended family was a way of life for us. Taking children, nurturing them to emotional health, is the call for walking in love.

Ephesians 5:2

"And walk in love, as Christ also hath loved us, and hath given himself for us an offering and a sacrifice to God for a sweetsmelling savour."

The move to Portland was more of obedience than sacrifice although it meant sharing our lives with desperate girls that we did not know. We refused to be foster parents. These girls needed to be parented like our own children for an extended time. It takes time to heal.

The first six girls we received into the home that we purchased in Portland were "the worst cases" the social worker informed us. One of the girls was a lesbian and did not trust men. Joshua was the first father she learned to love. Another girl was a fire setter and had an incestuous relationship with her father. A third girl was totally rejected by her mother and father, and we were her 13th family. One girl hung out in the streets prostituting. The fifth girl had been rejected by her stepmother and the father did not want her in the house. And the sixth girl had been molested in several foster homes and her mother was a prostitute.

21

It was God's grace that allowed us to parent those girls and several more after them. Joshua became a father to them, and my job became that of a listener and nurturer. We instituted family meetings as a way to encourage communication and dialogue. When each girl began to open up, some of their experiences were so devastating that I cried many times as I shared their pain.

One of the girls, Cassandra (not her real name), had to be talked to at least an hour each day before she would leave for school. She could not believe we could love her and had been diagnosed as "detached", never being able to bond. She was barely able to make a "D" in school. Most of her grades were F's. It took us a year to convince her that we truly loved her. Her testing was hard on us but we persevered.

Through receiving the attention she so desperately needed, Cassandra eventually became a leader in the house and helped us to keep order. Her grades went from a 1.0 grade point average to a 4.0 when she graduated from high school. Cassandra visits regularly at Christmas, and we hear from her periodically. She bonded to us and to two of our biological daughters. We are her family, although her mother finally accepted her after she was in her 2nd year of college.

Cassandra had to be prepared to receive us. It required a lot of time and love for her to believe that she could be accepted.

Bonding occurs in marriage when the relationship between the husband and wife is the priority and in the family when unconditional love and acceptance of each member, whether biological or otherwise, is practiced. In cases where children are part of the social service system, bonding can still occur when children are placed with families who are willing to accept them as part of their own family in the long term rather than short term foster care. The extended family process allows children to belong to someone who will connect to them permanently.

Reflections

When you think about the Belonging Chapter, meditate on the following:

How does bonding begin?

_____

_____

_____

_____

How do you know when you have bonded to someone?

_____

_____

_____

_____

Is bonding always necessary in a marriage relationship"
A friendship relationship?

_____

_____

_____

_____

Oh Lord, that my heart might be one with
Thine. The depths of which is love divine.
The oneness of such a union is beyond
my ability to imagine. But then oneness
with God is not imagination.
It is a relationship with my Father
the maker of all Creation.

O. Virginia Phillips
John 17:21

2

THE ONENESS CONNECTION

PEACE

When Joshua and I began teaching on "Oneness" we sensed that there was a revelation regarding the meaning of male and female as one flesh. Over the years we taught on the "one flesh" concept - two becoming one. We studied the book of Ephesians continually and it became increasingly clear that when Paul spoke of marriage he was speaking of a great mystery. He said in Ephesians 5:32, "This is a great mystery but I speak concerning Christ and the church." That statement indicated to us that marriage is a covenant styled after Christ and His body the church.

In the chapter on husbands and wives (Ephesians 5), husbands are admonished to love their wives even as Christ also loved the church and gave Himself for it. (Ephesians 5:25) The church was set apart as Christ's body and in Ephesians 5:28, husbands are told this. "So ought men to love their wives as their own bodies. He that loveth his wife loveth himself."

This love referred to here is not an Eros, a sensual expression or philia a friendship relationship. This is agape, the unconditional love that Christ has for His own body of believers, the church. In marriage we become one flesh. We also read in Ephesians 5:30 that we are members of His (Christ's) body, of His flesh and His bones. This takes us back to Genesis 2:22 after the Lord God made a woman for Adam and brought her to him (Genesis 2:23).

And Adam said, *"This is now bone of my bones, and flesh of my flesh: …"*

This is an illustration of the church. We believe, in God's mind, the church began when He created a male and a female. In them is the ability to reproduce. Through this reproduction process come the children of God, the body of Christ.

Because the marriage relationship is styled after the church whatever commandments are given for the church are also given to the man and wife. As members of the body of Christ, we are to leave all our carnal ways and cleave (be joined) to Christ. We believe that is where the expression "join the church" originated to be joined to Christ.

In Genesis 2:24 we read,

"Therefore shall a man leave his father and mother, and shall cleave unto his wife and they shall be one flesh."

Mark 10:7 states so they are no more twain, but one flesh." From the very beginning of creation God made them male and female. (Mark 10:6) They were created to become one. Although Adam was created first, God took part of his flesh to fashion woman. Adam became Eve's covering, her protector.

In several scriptures, i.e.,1 Corinthians 6-7 and Ephesians 5, there is a parallel regarding the body of Christ and the joining of the body of man and wife- Christ paid a great price for us... therefore glorify God in your body, and in your spirit which are God's. In 1 Corinthians 7:4 we read,

"The wife hath not power of her own body, but the husband: and likewise also the husband hath not power of his own body, but the wife."

In 1 Corinthians 6:19 we read a similar passage for the church,

"What? know ye not that your body is the temple of the Holy Ghost which is in you, which ye have of God, and ye are not your own."

A marriage union becomes one flesh but he that is joined unto the Lord is one spirit. (1 Corinthians 6:17).

"Oneness" is God's desire for marriage and for His church. He was so desirous of oneness that He prayed to the Father in John 17:21,

"That they all may be one; as thou, Father, art in me, and I in thee, that they also may be one in us: that the world may believe that thou hast sent me."

He was speaking about the disciples, but in verse 20 Jesus said,

"Neither pray I for these alone, but for them also which shall believe on me through their words;"

He is speaking of His church.

The mystery Paul is speaking of in Ephesians 5:32 for the marriage relationship is based on the perfection of Jesus' relationship with the church. Is it any wonder that satan's design is to destroy marriage, for this covenant between a man and his wife is a covenant between two people who when married are no longer two but one. And we are members of Christ's body, of His flesh and of His bones. We are His bride.

As Christians, Christ is the head of the marriage relationship and we are to be led by Him as His heirs - connected to Him in spirit as sons. (Romans 12:14).

Jesus was there with His Father in the very beginning. They were of one mind and one spirit. This is the state that man and wife should aspire to imitate. Although man and wife become one flesh– in Christ they are also one spirit. In every instance from the very beginning, God gave man a spiritual plan to follow because God's

27

children are spiritual. In Christ, all the fullness of Deity dwelt in bodily form in Him. We have been made complete in Christ and He is the head over all. We also see the completeness of man when God created them male and female for Adam was not complete without Eve.

Man and wife were created to become one flesh. This explains why males have some female hormones and females have some male hormones; although the dominant hormones determine the gender. Sharing some of each hormone affords man the ability to be sensitive to the emotions of his wife and the wife to be sensitive to the needs and emotions of her husband. We were created to understand our spouses.

This union is modeled after the relationship between God and His Son Jesus. When God breathed into Adam's nostrils, he received life. God's Spirit is life. The oneness that God intends for a man and his wife cannot be attained without the indwelling Spirit of God. The model for this oneness was in the very beginning when God created man in perfection. We can only obtain this perfection through the perfect one, Jesus.

The oneness we have seen in man and wife from the beginning we call the "one flesh" concept. Adam and Eve were of one flesh.

"For as the woman is of the man, even so is the man also by the woman; but all things of God." (1 Corinthians 11: 12)

The institution of marriage occurred when Adam received Eve by saying in Genesis 2:23,

"And Adam said, This in now bone of my bones, and flesh of my flesh: she shall be called Woman, because she was taken out of Man."

Here the woman is a type of the church, the bride of Christ. (Ephesians 5:25-32) We are the church because we are in Christ.

This bond of perfection in the beginning is also found In the

New Testament as a reaffirmation or God's plan for marriage as model of the church. In God, all things are balanced in both the spiritual and natural. Man can understand naturally the closeness in a marriage relationship. The experience of a loving relationship in marriage can bring man to an understanding of the relationship of Christ and the church by the revelation of' the Holy Spirit through the scriptures.

As earlier stated in the section on bonding, like two pieces of paper glued together, once the bond is set, to tear it apart will mutilate the original paper and render it marred and in pieces. This is what happens when two people who have bonded then divorce. You cannot separate one flesh without scarring the body, spirit and emotion of the couple. The cleaving is part of the bonding process in a relationship. This means to set aside all other relationships as priorities and the husband and wife become each other's priority.

This cleaving and bonding, which brings oneness, is the same expectation that Christ has of us when we become one with Him. In Mark 10:29, 30 it states,

> *"... Verily I say unto you, there is no man that hath left house, or brethren, or sisters, or father, or mother, or wife, or children, or lands, for my sake, and the gospel's, But he shall receive an hundredfold now in this time, houses, and brethren, and sisters, and mothers, and children, and lands, ..."*

Notice this verse does not state that he will receive wives.

The institution of marriage is such an honorable one that God has used it to illustrate the church. All scriptures relating to the church can also relate to the marriage relationship between man and wife. It is God's way of teaching us how wonderful a marriage relationship can be.

Marriages are being shaken just as the church is being shaken today. There is a direct correlation between the problems in marriages and the problems in the church. Both are experiencing tremendous upheaval. We know what is happening in the churches by the statistics on divorce.

There is also a falling away in church attendance and commitment to Christ. However, churches that provide strong teaching on marriage and the family as the foundation of the Christian church are growing and broken marriages are being healed. We have experienced this while visiting churches of various denominations. We have seen the unity that has come in churches where marriages are being strengthened.

This oneness in the marriage relationship encompasses every aspect including the way a man and woman respond to each other's body. In marriage, the woman's body is no longer solely hers nor is the man's body solely his. "The wife hath not power over her own body, but the husband, and likewise also the husband hath not power over his own body, but the wife." (1 Corinthians 7:4).

We are taught in Ephesians 5:28-29,

"So ought men to love their wives as their own bodies. He that loveth his wife loveth himself. For no man ever yet hated his own flesh; but nourisheth and cherisheth it, even as the Lord the church:"

A man is to love his wife's body as he does his own. He does not batter or abuse his own body nor should he batter or abuse his wife's body because they are one flesh.

A man who deliberately batters himself can be declared insane. A man who batters his wife is also insane, for according to the scripture, he is the savior of the wife's body. (Ephesians 5:23) A husband who understands this role as protector of his wife's body will not deliberately hurt himself or anyone in his household.

An example of the one flesh concept can be explained by an occurrence in our counseling offices several years ago. Although we can provide many examples, this one illustrates how marriage is affected adversely by infidelity. A lady in her early 30's began counseling with Joshua and, after three visits, she confided that she thought her husband was having an illicit affair with another woman. When she was asked what proof she had said she had none, that it was a strong emotional impression.

She said her husband didn't spend weekends away from home, he provided financially for the family, he even attended church with them, but she still felt something was wrong even though their sex life was still normal. She was depressed for no apparent reason and felt a lack of self-worth. I encouraged her to begin thinking of all the right things that were happening in the marriage and provided some advice to give her esteem a boost.

On the fourth visit, her husband came· and was counseled separately. After the second session with him, Joshua asked him (since all sessions are confidential) if he was having an affair. He was taken aback, and paused for a moment before he blushed and said slowly, "Yes, I have been seeing another woman for six years." But he assured Joshua that his family was not adversely affected. He said, "I have my home life under control."

This affair began as a simple luncheon date with a client (he is a lawyer) and continued into a relationship that he had not been able to break up. When Joshua told him what was happening with his wife and explained the "one flesh" concept to him, he was amazed. Whenever a married man has sex with another woman he is using his wife's body also, because his body belongs to her. (1 Corinthians 7:4) They are no longer two in the flesh but one.

Although his wife had no proof he was having an affair, she felt it in her body and in her emotions. She was not complete. In essence, part of her body was being used in an illicit affair. Once the "one flesh" concept is understood, we can recognize how the fabric of relationships are torn by infidelity.

31

This man broke off his relationship with the other woman and began appreciating his wife more. She discontinued her counseling almost immediately after her husband ended his affair. She confided, "I don't know what happened or what you said in your sessions with him, but he is different." Her body was complete now because her husband was no longer sharing himself with someone else. Once a couple understands the concept of one flesh, their marriage is less susceptible to infidelity.

A happy marriage and family begins with the understanding of the roles that the husband and wife have in their marriage relationship. When Jesus is the head of the home there is an accountability process that operates within the household. The husband is the head of the wife and they both instruct and teach the children, in agreement. If something is not working in the family, the head of the home (Jesus) should be consulted by both husband and wife.

There is a mutual submission in a marriage in all things especially in the sexual relationship. Sex on demand is not a loving way to approach such a special union. This special time must be paved with preparation, which requires sensitivity, understanding, gentleness and open communication.

A wife and husband who demonstrate oneness in their home impart this principle to their children. Children observe so much of the teaching of one flesh by the way their parents speak to and touch one another'. "Oneness" must be practiced in the home as part of the natural flow of a happy family.

Reflections

What does it mean that the man is the savior of his wife's body?

_____

_____

_____

_____

_____

What does cleaving mean in the cultivation of marriage?_____

_____

_____

_____

_____

_____

If you are reading this book before marriage, what is your understanding of "oneness?"

_____

_____

_____

_____

_____

_____

Friendship is so important in a lasting relationship. It is the foundation upon which the intimate bond between two people is developed.

O. Virginia Phillips
Ecclesiastes 4:9-10

3

THE FRIENDSHIP CONNECTION

GENTLENESS

I have experienced the presence of God for as long as I can remember. Even when I was alone and wanted a person to talk to, I had no fear. I would read my Bible or dream large, seemingly impossible dreams or talk to my friend, Jesus. The first book I ever read, at age 3, was the Bible.

God has taught me what a true friend is. Friends don't forsake you when you need them. We became so close after I was widowed with eight children that I listened then as never before. I had no one else to whom I could confide my deepest feelings. During that time, God became my spiritual husband, my friend and my confidante. I had a close relationship with Him.

Each month all of our expenses were met and my faith was more than a belief, it was a gift. Perhaps it was during this time that I began to understand how near my heart was to God. I certainly began to know Him for myself, not only as someone to pray to and trust, but as someone who would listen to me and understand. During this time, Joel 2:12 was so real,

> *"Therefore, also now, saith the Lord, turn to me with all your heart and with fasting and with weeping and with mourning ... ."*

Our fellowship was not broken, but my heart was and He bound it up and healed it.

I knew no one else could help me through this time, although there were those who tried. I knew they loved me, but they were not there nights when I could not sleep and mornings when I awakened not knowing what the day would bring. My children needed care so I could not return to my teaching position at the university, and I had no visible means of income. But I never thought of applying for public assistance.

I relied on the only friend I knew, I became intimate with God. For months when I awakened in the mornings, the same six birds would sing at my window while I talked to my friend, Jesus. It took awhile to realize that God sent the birds to comfort me. I didn't have a grief support group, but I had instructions. I was not sure each day what scripture I should read, but when I opened my Bible there would be encouraging words for that day. Each day I was fed the right word for that day.

During this time, several of the children became deathly ill and I had no medical insurance. Three of my four sons had measles, mumps and chicken pox all at the same time, which was very unusual. They had swollen testicles, and they were in such poor condition they could have become infertile. My second oldest daughter was found to have only one functioning kidney after an examination by a physician friend who checked her thoroughly due to a bladder weakness. There was no one but my friend, Jesus who could advise me on how to treat each of them.

I kept the boys as quiet as I could and allowed very little light into their room because their eyes were almost swollen shut from the combination of chicken pox and mumps. I gave them warm milk and put calamine lotion on them daily, and I prayed. My friend Jesus healed them completely without a mark on their bodies. And only one of them had a testicle problem that was so minor that it did not interfere with his fathering children. All the boys have married and have children of their own.

My daughter Linda has both kidneys functioning by divine intervention. A doctor who lived down the hill from us agreed to treat her. I had begun to give her medication and had decided that she needed surgery so that the one good kidney would remain functional. On the way to the hospital for observation, God healed her dysfunctional kidney. I had been praying all along, but that morning I was so impressed to be specific and refuse surgery. I decided to do just that and called the doctor. He insisted that I bring her in. After a thorough examination, a bewildered doctor told me to keep her on medication just in case the test proved wrong. I didn't give her any more medication and the tests were correct. My daughter has two healthy kidneys.

My faith in my Friend took me to Him day after day. I asked Him what I should wear, what I should eat, all without fret or anxiety because 1 knew He would answer. This season in our relationship lasted one year. So when He said to pack up the children and move to a place I had never lived and had no friends, 1 packed up and moved.

He had taught me to rely on Him day after day, hour after hour. My friend taught me how faith works. This experience and many more—too numerous to mention here—happened in Healdsburg, California. Afterward, the children and I moved to Portland, Oregon

Friendship in marriage is a basic ingredient to maintaining harmony in the relationship. Harmony in marriage is under attack as never before. Most of this is due to a shift in traditions, knowledge and understanding of family relationships. The traditional pattern for marriage has been assimilated in social and cultural perspectives that support the rights of individuals rather than the interdependence of family members.

The traditional family had well-defined male and female roles.

It was understood that the man was the head and made the major decisions; he was the financial provider and protector. The wife was submissive to her husband, a homemaker and child rearer. Children were expected to be respectful and obedient to parents.

Religion was a very important part of the family life as well as the extended family. Family members were nearby and supportive. They loved and provided financial and spiritual support when needed. In comparison, the contemporary family is isolated from these traditions. As a result, generations are growing up without the knowledge of traditional values that hold families together.

Expectation for marriage is often based on feelings, which is a major cause of divorce in young marriages. Individuals marry to get their needs met but they seldom identify what their needs are to one another prior to marriage. Dating has replaced friendships. The result of this lack of awareness of the opposite sex as friends establishes romantic love relationships based on "feelings" rather than commitment. Friendship is foundational to respect, communication and love.

In Christian relationships, friendship is the foundation upon which the intimate bond between two people is developed. When Joshua and I prepared a couple for marriage, one of the first subjects we began with is friendship. A friend is one who is a burden bearer when the load is too heavy for one alone. A friend is long suffering enough to carry the weight until the other is able to carry it.

A friend when communicating puts his/her whole self into the conversation (Exodus 33:11). Friends speak face to face, eye to eye and listen to one another without outside interference. Friends have covenant relationships and love each other as themselves (1 Samuel 18:3). In the closeness of knitted souls, a friend defers to the other; when they disagree, they are not disagreeable (1 Samuel 18:1). A friend edifies and, if necessary, lays his/her life down for the other (John 15:13).

Friends are true and unchangeable. (Proverbs 17:17) Friends arc dependent upon one another and will give advice, are non-judgmental and there when they are needed. You can relax with a friend and enjoy acceptance.

A husband and wife can learn to be sensitive to one another and build a firm foundation by utilizing "transference." They can experience each other's heartfelt needs. Transference involves the woman sensing the needs of her husband; in essence, being the husband for a session and the husband sensing his wife's needs by being the wife for a session. Each shares the other's emotions. Friendship causes a couple to strive toward intimate communication and sharing in all areas of their lives.

So much of my teenage years was spent longing for a friend that I could trust, one with whom I could share my deepest feelings and know that he or she would not hurt me. I was blessed with such a friend when I met Joshua. He was so easy to talk to. I could share my weaknesses with him as easily as I shared my strengths and he was never critical.

I remember how faithful Jesus was whenever I need an answer in my relationship with Joshua. Joshua was my soul mate, the one I waited for and who God sent to me after I learned a few lessons over the years of heart connection with God.

The closeness of a friend should be the same closeness in a marriage. Friends are as close as brothers (Deuteronomy 13:6). When the wife or husband reaches an impasse in their relationship and thinks of leaving the marriage they should remember that they are connected by the blood of Jesus and you don't leave a brother or sister. Your wife or husband is your brother or sister in Christ. One of the reasons that our married children felt such security in Joshua's and my relationship was because we were friends. My children knew that friends remain in a relationship because their hearts are knit together.

It is healthy to develop friendship within one's own family to maintain relationships. It is also important to balance life with friends outside the immediate family. Close friends can help keep the balance in family relationships by providing wise counsel and support.

Some professional women are often too busy with their families, jobs and community work to cultivate friendships with other women besides those immediately available at church, work or in community service. But being part of a group with common interests sometimes resolves the problem of not having a close "sister" friend. I personally find that after relating to my family, my church, ministry and those people with whom I serve on various community-related projects, I seldom have the energy to cultivate a close, committed relationship with another person who is not already a priority in my life.

We should take inventory. Do we really have friends that we can call and with whom we can take a much needed mental break without having to rebuild the relationship? A friend who will listen and one who can be trusted to be honest and unaffected by status, prestige, profession or gender?

I must confess that having a husband who was my best friend resolved most of my outside sharing needs. But now I do have those moments when sharing with another woman would be wonderful. Sometimes I drop a personal note to women whom I admire. You could begin by planning to renew sagging relationships with at least two friends. Once a month is barely enough for a mental break with a friend, but it's a beginning. Remember, you can only commit to two or three friends but you can be friendly to everyone.

Reflections

Should friendship in marriage be based on feelings?
Why or why not?

_____

_____

_____

_____

_____

Can marriage bond without friendship?
Why or why not?

_____

_____

_____

_____

Can a marriage relationship be complete without friendship?
Why or why not?

_____

_____

_____

_____

_____

Commitment is a life test;
one in which we dare not rest
in mediocrity. It is the muscle
that holds us together
when our strength fails.

O. Virginia Phillips

4

THE COMMITMENT CONNECTION

LONG-SUFFERING

During my high school years in a Catholic boarding school, I learned from the nuns that there were two vocations I could choose and be happy: becoming a good wife and mother or becoming a good nun. I almost became a nun, but I chose being a wife and mother instead.

I believe I must have been born with a mother's heart. I didn't know how to parent because I had no models, but I did know how to love. I read everything I could on parenting but learned to practice what I read through day to day experiences. I learned some things by listening to the advice of older people about marriage and family.

Sister Albina, the nun at the boarding school would remind me, **"Whatever you do, commit totally to it and do your very best."** It never occurred to me that my marriage wouldn't work out or that my children wouldn't grow up together. Once my goals were set, I had to follow through.

Parenting became a great mountain to climb, and I loved to achieve my goals. I wanted to be the perfect mother, wife and career woman. I set out to do all three and learned that there is always a season for events to occur as they should. I had to learn how to be a wife and mother and wait for the right time for a career. I discovered that commitment takes courage.

A promise made in most marriages is to love and remain in the relationship through sickness and health, wealth or rags, hardships or joy. Marriage is a life test. 1 recall how I felt when I finally married Roy, my first husband. Ours was not an ideal, emotional, love-at-first sight feeling on my part. He decided that he wanted to marry me and would not stop wooing me. In fact, he respected me so much, we did not even kiss or cuddle during our friendship until the day I said, "Yes, I will marry you."

I knew so little about what a lifelong relationship really meant. I only knew that I could clean house and be faithful. Faithfulness is a virtue that has almost lost its value in today's society. It should be taught in every family.

A committed marital relationship is ordained by God. God wanted a family so he commanded Adam and Eve to replenish the earth. His commitment is so strong to His family, the church, it is bone of His bone and flesh of His flesh (Ephesians 5:30), the same words that Adam used to describe Eve. God's commitment to His body, the church, is the same today as it was in the beginning. His example of commitment is to be our example in marriage. He will never leave nor forsake us.

I learned commitment early. I think my mother taught me by example. I learned that whatever you start to do - commit to it wholeheartedly. It takes courage to commit, to connect with someone you think you know, only to discover later that you are so different. (God performed that miracle in my first marriage).

I have to admit that one of the reasons I married is because I was tired of being alone, poor and having so little support. Little did I realize that God purposed this in my life because He was to be the only reality I had. The integrity taught me by the nuns, the compassion learned from the priest, the importance of hard work

44

imparted to me by my mother, and the promise she spoke to me that I was a special person kept me through life's tests. These gave me the resilience to hang in with my marriage and to learn the lessons of motherhood.

I remember reading somewhere that the tests of life are to make not break us. Trouble may demolish a man's business but will build up his character. The blow at the outward man may be the greatest blessing to the inner man. If God then puts or permits anything hard in our lives, be sure that the real peril, the real trouble, is that we shall lose if we flinch or rebel.

The day Roy proposed was the day I had eaten my last hot dog, and I had only 49 cents left to eat for that week. I needed $100 for books that my scholarship didn't cover, and I was tired from working and studying. I needed a break and since I met Roy, I had decided not to enter the convent. He said that day, and I shall never forget it, "If you marry me, you will eat steak."

It was two years before that promise came true. His mother cooked a steak for us. Our first baby was born the first year of our marriage. His job did not make ends meet, and we ended up in a low-income housing complex. Thank God, it was a new one in the suburbs.

I remember one Easter we had no food in the house. Roy went to a little store that remained open seven days a week including holidays. He asked the owner if he could work for food. Roy bought home a bag of food and we had a great dinner—with leftovers for two days.

The first five years were difficult ones, but the joy of being together and the responsibility of parenting four children in five years kept us focused. There was never a thought of separation. Our commitment to each other and to the children was final.

Commitment is the entrusting, joining and connecting of one

person to another person. When a man and a woman commit themselves in marriage they must recognize the totality of the union. They become one flesh, one body. Commitment is to cherish and nurture another and not to seek your own way.

A committed marriage relationship revolves around an understanding that divorce is not an option. Life springs out of a committed relationship because each partner dies to selfishness. Total commitment is a lofty goal and seemingly unattainable in this society. However, it occurs within the spirit and is a mindset. It is not moved by social or cultural circumstances, and it knows no color or race. A Christian's commitment to his or her spouse is directly connected to the spirit of commitment in Christ.

How can this spiritual strategy be implemented considering the day-to-day marital conflicts and social conditioning? We must first understand the marriage relationship in balance. In every instance of creation, there is a balance. There is also a hierarchy and balance in a marriage relationship: Jesus, man, wife and offspring.

When Jesus is not the head of a marriage it is off-balance. When the wife regards children as a priority over her husband, it brings an imbalance. The perfect trinity in marriage is Jesus-husband-wife. When these three are in the proper place children learn and grow through this model.

Man has to understand that he was created in the image of God to glorify Him. If we concentrate on the worldly models of marriages, we forget who we are. God created man and breathed life into him. We belong to Him. In 1 Corinthians 6:19, Paul speaking to the Corinthian church says, "What? Know ye not that your body is the temple of the Holy Spirit which is in you, which ye have of God, and ye are not your own?"

Unless we realize the responsibility and the job of this identity, we become self-centered and waver off into excuses: "I am the way I am because of my parents," or "I must fornicate because it's expected of me," or "If I am submissive, I'll seem henpecked." These are among the numerous excuses given when total commitment is not a priority in the marriage.

There are cultural, traditional and social norms that remain a prevalent part of our marriage behavior that must be eliminated when they are opposed to the word of God. God's word is life. It breaks down barriers, sheds light in the dark areas of our lives, and sets us free when the bondage of tradition and culture opposes our commitment to our spouse.

During one of our counseling sessions with a beautiful, intelligent and very aware couple in their early 30's, we were asked by the husband, "How do I handle it when the guys ask me what I do in my free time? Actually I enjoy being home playing with the kids. I even enjoy cleaning the house, but I can't tell them. They will laugh me right out of the conversation." The young woman, on the other hand, enjoyed her job and the stimulating conversations of others in her profession. She wouldn't be happy "just being a housewife."

As a result, she attended meetings connected with her work two evenings a week while her husband stayed home. They had agreed on these arrangements and, on the surface, seemed happy with their decision. But outside pressures and their traditional upbringing was causing conflict in their relationship. Both were feeling guilty about their agreement.

We could have counseled them on positive communication and acceptance of their situation. But we had to provide the basic information on commitment and relationship from a Biblical base because the couple professed Christ. A committed relationship is based on love and respect for each other's talents. This couple needed to take their concentration off what others thought and place it on each other's needs, as well as the basic needs of their children. Their first commitment had to be made totally to Christ and then to each other. We know we are "bought with a price" therefore glorify God in your body and in your spirit, which are God's (1Corinthians 6:20)

What about the case of a non-believer married to a believer? The commitment is the same. Christ died for us when we were yet in our sins. (Romans 5:8) We must remember our own behavior in choosing a mate. Did we ask God for our partner? (1 Corinthians 7:12 says, "If any brother hath a wife that believeth not and she be pleased to dwell with him, let him not put her away." The same applied to the man in verse 13. Did we wait for God's answer or did we marry the one we wanted? If God places two Christians together, there is no reason for a lack of total commitment.

Commitment is not dependent on feelings. There are times in the marriage relationship when one spouse or both do not feel "in love." This is the time to remember the commitment and the times when loving feelings were there. Commitment means saying to oneself, "I do not feel loving but I am loved," and begin to show love by the act of the will. It is the outworking of the life in Christ Jesus.

Commitment in marriage must come in direct relationship to our commitment to Christ. A man and a woman bring to a relationship their strengths and weaknesses from childhood and, unless these seasons in their lives are dealt with thoroughly before marriage, they will be repeated in the marriage relationship.

When two people marry they covenant with God. Such a covenant should not be taken lightly. Oftentimes, couple's divorce because they don't like each other, not thinking of the seriousness of the covenant between God and themselves. All things are possible to them who believe (Mark 9:23). Excellent marriages are possible when the roles and relationships are defined by the word of God. All answers to marriage conflict can be found in His Word.

There are several reasons why marriages are experiencing inordinate conflict. Some involve an unevenly yoked relationship where one partner is a believer and the other is a non-believer. The burden falls upon the Christian partner since he or she is the one who carries the weight of understanding the word of God and maintaining the attitude that draws the non-believer to Christ. (1 Corinthians 7:14) In this case, God's grace is sufficient, and the believer can submit to Christ, commit the marriage to Him and commit to the marriage relationship. Often marriage conflict is brought upon the believer because of disobedience to the scripture

"Be ye not unevenly yoked," (2 Corinthians 6: 14):

This may have happened because of a lack of teaching, or selfishness or simply wanting one's own way. When two unbelievers marry and one becomes a Christian but the other remains an unbeliever, by committing the marriage relationship to Christ, they can be unified. This might not occur immediately, but patience is a virtue that must be exercised in a marriage relationship.

"And whatsoever ye do, do it heartily, as to the Lord, ..." Colossians 3:23.

Marriage, like the church, is a living organism. The life of a marriage, as in the church, is mutually supplied. It not only consumes energy but also gives it. When one partner suffers, both suffer; when one is joyous, so is the other. Because of this commitment, one partner can fulfill the needs of the other. (Colossians 1:24)

Sowing and reaping is a principle that works for anyone. Whatever a man sows that he also reaps, whether positive or negative. If a spouse does not feel loving, demonstrate love anyway through the things you do for the other person. Take stock of what you desire in your marriage and begin to sow the seed in your spouse. The scripture tells us, in Galatians 6:7-9, to sow and verse 9 tells us not to be weary in well doing, for in due season, we shall reap, if we faint not. What a promise to the church and to married couples.

Marriage is a pilgrimage traveled in seasons. The fall journey is a season of change and brings new problems. In many marriages, changes are not anticipated, but we must realize that we grow and our expectations change as we grow and develop. Some couples operate off expectations that are years old, although their circumstances have changed numerous times. Without good communication, one spouse can grow and develop in areas the other doesn't realize. So when colors change in the fall, be reminded that needs and expectations also change in the seasons of life.

There is a winter journey in marriage when feelings aren't so loving. The winter season is a time for sowing love by loving without conditions attached and developing kindness by being kind even though you do not think the other person deserves it. Marriage is not based on who is the most deserving but on how much can be deposited into it to keep it growing and developing. When feelings grow cold, rekindling love relationship through the sowing process warms each person.

The winter season is a time when the relationship needs to rest from old expectations and new ones be developed through sensitivity and communication. This is a season to bond. Forgive all past hurts that are in your heart and mind. The winter season anticipates a new season so a continual planting of the seeds of unconditional love keeps hope alive.

In the spring journey of marriage, the seeds planted in the winter will spring up if we faint not. Marriage, like the church, needs to focus on the biblical principle of sowing and reaping. Understand that whatever we give will be returned if the motivation is pure. Christ, our example, loved the church so much that He gave Himself. Commitment is giving. In marriage, when a spouse is to the point where he or she feels there is nothing more to give, this is not the time to give up but to think about the spring season when what you have already planted will begin to sprout up showing new life.

Seasons are different for different people. This is because God knows us well and how long we need to remain in a season. This is why He tells us not to be weary in well doing, for in due season, we shall reap if we faint not. Everyone's spring season when the fruit begins to produce will come. Some seasons are longer than others, but the final product will be worth the effort we put into it. We can look forward to full fruitfulness in the summer season.

I often remember the life of my mentor and friend Vera Boudreaux, a missionary and evangelist. She was married to a man who was a good husband and father but was insensitive to her spiritual needs. He did not receive Christ until 18 years after she became a Christian. Yet she planted love by not nagging and by doing her wifely duties with joy because she knew that God's word never returns void.

She took every opportunity to do good toward her husband. As a result of her planting in the winter season, she is now reaping a harvest of abundance. They were partners on the mission field and were married for more than 50 years. Her winter season produced patience because she was able to exercise her faith in God's word. When the testing comes, we must recognize that we have an opportunity to build our marriage in that season.

James 1:3-4 tells us that when we face various trials, we are to count it all joy,

> **"... Knowing this,** (not thinking or wondering this, but it is a fact) **that the trying of your faith worketh patience. But let patience have her perfect work, ..."**

We will mature in our marriage relationship when we exercise faith and patience.

Joshua believed and I believe that a marriage can be perfect (mature) when we use these principles of love and commitment and are steadfast in our belief that God's word is true. We will reap if we faint not.

A Season of Listening

I listen as you speak, Holy Spirit; my heart is
open to hear Your words for Your words are sweet.
They bring life to my soul. I proclaim again the
good news that you deliver your people daily
from our enemies. I reverence You, my
Redeemer and King. I will rejoice in You.

Thank You for
your unfailing love and
Your everlasting mercy.

A prayer taken from **30 Days of Prayer** *by the author.*

Reflections

Can commitment be enough without a marriage ceremony?

_____

_____

_____

_____

_____

If one person is committed and the other is not, can the marriage continue? _____

_____

_____

_____

_____

Can a nonbeliever have the same commitment in marriage as a believer? _____

_____

_____

_____

_____

_____

Submission is a misunderstood word which,
when practiced in reality, can bring us to
great depths of understanding and propel
us to great heights of wisdom, with a
sudden attitude adjustment.

O. Virginia Phillips

5

THE SUBMISSION CONNECTION
SELF-CONTROL

Submission is a Biblical principle that finds its basis in an attitude exemplified by Jesus Himself. For, though He was equal with God, He submitted Himself to God in all things (Philippians 2:6). Jesus chose to submit Himself to the will of the Father so that the purposes of God might be realized. Submission is not an inferior position because Jesus knew the mind of the Father and this was the authority upon which His ministry on earth was based.

The principle that Jesus established for us to follow is one of yielding and surrender, but we must, as He did, know the mind of the Father. When we know the Father's wishes submission is not painful. The Father provides us with the tools we need to act according to His will. In the marriage relationship, the couple is provided a clear directive from God, a commandment that cannot be changed by man's social conditioning or tradition.

Too often women have come under bondage because of the emphasis on submission, which sometimes requires them to forget their own personalities and become doormats. However, everyone, male and female, receives the same commandment,

> *"Submitting yourselves one to another in the fear of God."*
> (Ephesians 5:21)

Wives are then given the directive for submission:

> *"Wives, submit yourselves unto your own husbands, as unto the Lord."* (Ephesians 5:22)

This submission to the husband as to the Lord recognizes that Jesus is the head of the husband and when a wife chooses to submit to her husband she is also submitting to the Father. By understanding this, a woman can go to her husband's Father (God) knowing that He will speak to her husband as she brings her problems and desires to Him. It frees the wife from trying to coerce her husband into doing some of the things she feels he should be doing to fulfill his role as leader in the home.

Submission is not servitude or slavery. It does not suggest that a woman is inferior or insignificant. She is the most important person in her husband's life. She is a partner, companion, lover and friend. She is the completion of her husband. Biblical submission does not stifle initiative or limit a wife in any way.

God, in His wisdom, actually frees the woman through submission. He places a great responsibility upon the husband to bring about this obedience in his wife. He commands the husband to love his wife even as Christ also loved the church, and gave Himself for it,

> *"That he might sanctify and cleanse it with the washing of the water by the word,"* (Ephesians 5:26)

A husband must be the spiritual head of his household and bring the word of God to his wife and children. By this act, God gave the mantle of priesthood to the husband.

The marriage relationship is like a garden. In a garden, weeds grow up among the good plants and they must be plucked out or else they will choke out the crop. This is an ongoing task. We cannot wait until the harvest is all grown. Care must be provided daily. The same principle applies to the marriage. Cultivating a marriage relationship requires diligence and perseverance, daily pruning and sowing. If a man or woman wants a certain harvest from a marriage, he/she must first plant the seed.

The scripture teaches the husband,

"...let every one of you in particular so love his wife even as himself; and the wife see that she reverence her husband." (Ephesians 5:33)

The implementation of this comes by practicing sowing and reaping. In order for a husband to be properly revered as priest of his household, it is imperative that he plants the seed of love in his garden. A marriage can be a garden of love, joy, respect, gentleness, kindness and longsuffering. All these are pleasurable to harvest, but love must be planted first in the home in order for the harvest to be gathered.

So much has been written on submission in the context of acts of obedience, which constitutes "works." Actually, submission is not "works." Works are the result of submission. Submission is an attitude of surrender, a yielding of oneself to the need of another. This is total yielding, which makes the other person the priority. In marriage, this total submission or heart attitude cannot be totally accomplished unless the heart is first totally yielded to Christ.

Christ is the example of total submission. He obeyed the Father willingly and without restraint. If we are to be submissive, we must understand what the will of the Lord is for marriage and be filled with His Spirit to practice it. The flesh is not submissive of itself; it must be brought under subjection to the will of God. The scripture tells us in Ephesians 5:20 that we are to give thanks always for all things unto God, the Father, in the name of our Lord Jesus Christ. When husbands and wives are obedient to Him, then they can submit themselves one to another in fear (reverence) of God. Submission then becomes a mutual attitude for both husband and wife.

Wives are to submit themselves unto their own husbands as unto the Lord. Submission pays dividends, it dictates sacrifice and heaps kindness upon the head of the recipient. Even though the scripture speaks to the wife concerning being subject to her husband, it clearly states that husband and wife are to submit themselves to one another, thus making each other their priority.

The portion of scripture so often overlooked is

Ephesians 5:23 (NIV), *"For the husband is head of the wife as Christ is head of the church, His body, of which He is the Savior."*

This is a serious responsibility on the part of the husband, to love his wife even Christ also loves the church. A husband who loves his wife this way will receive his wife's submission, which flows out of a perfect love relationship.

The love of Christ in a man flows into his wife; a nurturing, protecting, saving, cherishing love that edifies and builds up his spouse. The submissive heart of a woman will choose to be subject to her husband. She is subject "to her own husband." She is not subject, as some men think to all males, only to her husband who is one with her and can love her as Christ loves the church.

Submission of the wife to the husband "as unto the Lord" is a position that the church finds herself in as she (the church) reverences Christ. This beautiful relationship between husband and wife is of the highest order and is what Paul refers to in

Ephesians 5:32 *"... but I speak concerning Christ and the church."*

Christ never forces us into submission; He gently woos and calls us into surrender through His great love for us.

Submission springs forth from a woman out of the warmth she feels in her heart for her husband. The catalyst is his love for her and love cultivates respect. The husband's love for his wife is the most fundamental principle in marriage relations. There again it points to Christ. The same unconditional love that Christ shows the church is expected of the husband. Husbands should ask Christ for this selfless attitude toward their spouse. The result of such a desirous love enables the husband to protect and honor his wife, speak well of her and be a loyal husband and friend. A submitted, responsive, loyal and loving wife will reverence a husband like this.

For almost five years, as a widow, I made my own decisions, disciplined my children without a second opinion and had the freedom of movement without the responsibility of pleasing a partner. Although sometimes I yearned for an adult companion, I enjoyed the freedom after almost 20 years of marriage to my first husband.

The first year of my marriage to Joshua, we talked about everything in order to know one another without any hidden thing. Joshua's love and patience won my heart. He had made a major transition himself. His wife passed away after more than 30 years of marriage. He moved to a different state to be with me. He inherited a wife and eight children along with another child that I was parenting for a single mother, and he had no friends of his own in this new town.

Joshua made a complete life change at age 54. His love for me was God inspired. Because I saw and experienced his love in so many ways, I knew he would never deliberately hurt me. Therefore, submission was an honor for me. It didn't occur immediately. Although my attitude was submissive, my old habits were still there. Without realizing it I kept taking charge of certain things. Joshua was very patient with me. When I disciplined the children he never once said "no." Gradually he encouraged me to let go and allow him to discipline by pointing out how quickly the children responded when he spoke.

Joshua didn't speak quickly but was quiet and watchful. When he spoke about a problem that a child had he had all the evidence and the solution. This taught me a great lesson in humility and I learned to respect Joshua as a total person. We became a team the first year, and we began ministering to families as on-call counselors. We discovered early on to pray in agreement. Some of the important lessons that I learned by practicing submission to my husband will work in any home where Jesus is Lord.

I learned to influence my husband for good. In obedience to 1 Peter 3:1, I spoke well of my husband to him and to others. My conversation was geared toward building up Joshua and encouraging him. There was no intentional criticism. If I wanted to change something he was doing, I spoke to him about how great I felt when he did it differently, while appreciating his efforts. Appreciation is a great influence in marriage. It builds up a spouse's confidence.

I learned to submit to Joshua in the areas that I wanted him to submit to me. This is the principle of sowing and reaping. I learned to speak of difficult situations only when he was rested, light-hearted and ready to listen. I sought his opinion and, even though I didn't always agree, I would respectfully listen.

I learned early in marriage to respect the position of my husband. I studied the word to find out what that meant. The Bible tells us that the husband is the head of the wife even as Christ is the head of the church (Ephesians 5:23). There is an order in marriage. When Joshua was slow to act as priest in our household I went to Jesus, his head, and in most cases, he submitted. It was not necessary to repeat myself over and over. After awhile, Joshua knew that I went to God because he changed in ways that would have been too difficult for most men on their own.

THE SUBMISSION CONNECTION – SELF-CONTROL

The principles in scripture really work when we are willing to wait on God. The words spoken in 1 Peter 3:1-7 should be practiced in marriage for they are true for every believer. When we speak of marriage we are using it as Paul did in Ephesians 5:32, **"This is a great mystery"** as an example of Jesus' relationship with the church.

Submission in the marriage relationship affects the obedience of children in the family. The first foundational teaching for children is obedience. Obedience to parents sets the relationship of' the child to God. The first commandment with promise is found in Ephesians 6:1-3,

> *"Children, obey your parents in the Lord for this is right. Honor thy father and mother that it may be well with thee and thou mayest live long on the earth."*

To submit to parents is to submit to God, for parents are responsible to rear children in the admonition of the Lord so that they may grow up with the understanding that they were created to worship and obey Him. This principle of submission is true for single heads of households where there is only one parent. A family changes, but God's word stands for any family whether both parents are there or not.

Delinquency is a problem in and to society. Education for some children has, at best, a band-aid effect. Too often school becomes a babysitting service rather than an opportunity for learning. The solution doesn't come easily. However, while the number of delinquents is growing, there are numerous young people who are turning to God for help.

Each human service provider involved in the care, nurture and development of delinquents has blamed others for the condition of these children. Parents often blame the schools, human service providers blame the parents and the enigmatic circle continues. However, no group has found a permanent and workable solution. The fact of the matter is that everyone - parents, schools and human service providers - must bear some responsibility for the outcome of these children.

Let us look at some of the ways each group can provide alternative ways to reconstruct the path of a delinquent child. After more than 45 years of working with parents and children, I firmly believe parents have the greatest influence on their children. Therefore, the family holds a crucial key to unlocking a child's learning potential and shaping a child into being a productive member of society. If parents continually reinforce a loving, nurturing, well-developed value system, the child, even if he chooses a delinquent path, may return to that value system when he matures.

However, delinquency is not something that occurs exclusively as a result of a negative home environment. It is the result of an unhealthy balance in a child's home, school and/or community life. Of course, if a child develops in a positive home environment, the risk is lower that the child will become delinquent. Schools can enhance a child's development or diminish his/her effectiveness.

Parents should rear their children with strong, positive values of obedience to authority and respect for others. However, if a child enters school where their teachers label them on a stereotypical basis rather than on a knowledgeable and understanding basis, then that child can and oftentimes will become affected educationally for the rest of their lives.

Once a child is deemed delinquent and becomes "caught up in the system," that child will most likely retain that stigma for a lifetime, unless there is cooperative intervention by the parents and school administrators. Today's children are products of a society whose values have changed markedly due in part to divorce. But institutions have not changed fast enough to meet the needs of the "new adolescent." Unless a child is reared with love, discipline and security beginning in the womb, he or she can be unduly influenced by peers, media and many other distractions.

Parents need support and sometimes specialized training in the rearing of their children. They need this support from churches, schools, human service organizations and neighbors. At times parents also need to seek counseling for their children and listen to what the child has to say about his/her feelings. Parent support groups can also serve as an extended family. Such a group can provide solutions to parenting problems and help as advocates for parents and children at the school.

This chapter has covered submission in the marriage relationship and in the parent-child relationship. It is important that children understand early to submit to authority; otherwise it will be difficult to submit to God. Hebrews 13: 17 says,

"Obey them that have the rule over you, and submit yourselves: for they watch for your souls, as they that must give account, that they may do it with joy, and not with grief: for that is unprofitable for you."

When submission is taught and lived in the home, the character of a child submitted to parents becomes a child that will listen and obey teachers and the laws of the land.

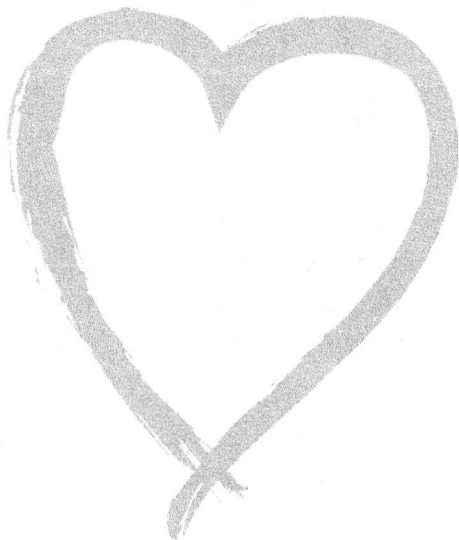

Reflections

To whom should we submit first in our marriage relationship?

_____

_____

_____

_____

_____

Does the word submission upset you? Why?

_____

_____

_____

_____

What is true submission in a marriage relationship?

_____

_____

_____

_____

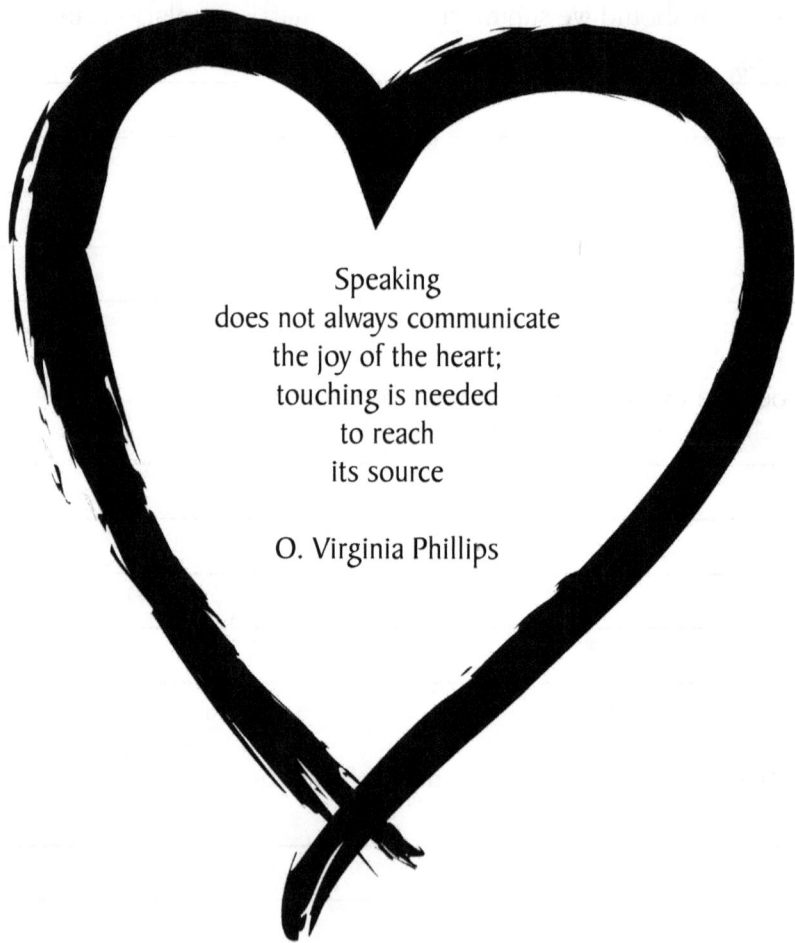

Speaking
does not always communicate
the joy of the heart;
touching is needed
to reach
its source

O. Virginia Phillips

6

THE COMMUNICATION CONNECTION

HOPE

My first husband, Roy, had a quiet, stoic disposition. He grew up in a household where he was the eldest. His mother was not demonstrative and he was given the task of caring for the house and his brothers after his stepfather died. Roy's background was Blackfoot and Cherokee Indian.

I am a vivacious person and I like to communicate. I felt his silence was strength and, before marriage, we talked. It didn't occur to me then that I would need to help him communicate more. After all, I had no marriage model except for the short time I lived with a stepfather that my mother later divorced.

I wanted a family so badly during those years I was alone, working my way through high school and college. I remember praying for a boyfriend to take me to the prom at my high school graduation. After high school, I met a couple of young men I wanted to have a relationship with but they became my friends instead and treated me like a sister.

I had been told that I was attractive and I believed I was, but I was also the studious type. I didn't hang with the crowd. I was always someone's best friend, someone to trust with secrets, but not to invite to the parties. So I had virtually no experience developing relationships with men. My time at St. Benedict the Moor was very rewarding and safe. The mother superior, Sister Albina, guided me in the principles of integrity and self-control and she, through conversation with me, increased my desire for higher education. Father Julian Phelan taught me the beauty of humility. He was so humble himself and he would talk to me about the importance of bowing before God in repentance. I watched him winter after winter when he would leave his office with his overcoat and galoshes and return with neither. He would say "I found a brother on the corner downtown that needed them worse than I did."

After completing high school at St. Benedict the Moor in 1954 I graduated valedictorian and worked that summer. I applied to the Cardinal Stritch College and received a scholarship with room and board the first year. I entered Cardinal Stritch College for Women in the fall of 1954. I was the only black girl there and the poorest but I had a goal in mind to get the highest degree possible. One of the nuns at the high school had taught me how to deal with stress and loneliness. It was a simple solution that she used for herself. She said, "Don't ever feel sorry for yourself. Simply lie down in a comfortable place, close your eyes and concentrate on something delightful and fall asleep. When you awake you will feel better." I practiced that especially my first year of college.

I worked in Milwaukee to pay for my personal needs. During the first summer of college, I was hired as a telephone representative. I was the only black person in that department. I didn't notice my racial difference as much as I noticed my longing to have a close friend with whom to communicate. I did meet a friend who roomed across from me in my dorm. Her name was Darlene Dlapa. She lived in a small town called Waukesha. Her neighbors were the Mitchell's, and she asked me to write her friend named Roy. He was in the Marine Corp. I wanted to write someone so we began writing each other.

Before Roy returned home I decided to enter the convent. My longing for a family was just that great. I hadn't seen my parents since I was 16. I had spent 2 years in college and I was 20 years old. I had planned to enter the convent in the fall but Roy returned home that summer. We started seeing each other. He took me to visit his family, and it became a regular Sunday date.

Except for his mother, I was the only female at the Sunday dinners and it felt good to be the center of someone's life. I had been lonely for a family for a long time. Even though I didn't want to get married and stop school, Roy constantly pursued me. He told my friend who introduced us that I was so green and naive that he was determined to marry me to save me from the world.

Roy and I eloped and started our life together in 1957. Little did I realize that we were both lonely people. Part of our agreement was that I would someday return to school. It was a learning experience for both of us from the beginning. Though we had both been lonely people, we learned and grew together.

Over 10 years, eight babies were born. We both wanted a family, but we hadn't talked about the number of children. Somewhere in my heart, I wanted to be the perfect wife and mother, but I had no blueprint. What I did have were research skills, so I read everything I could get my hands on about parenting but very little about marriage.

My desire for friendship helped me with my husband. Although we met other people, we became each other's best friend. I met other people through church, at the children's school and in the community. In fact, I was determined to have our children grow up in a good community where I knew the neighbors and the teachers at the schools.

I think I must have received my adult conversations through the avenues of church, school and community. I learned to communicate with my husband by connecting to his heart and studying his mannerisms. I learned when he needed to talk and what he was thinking by his responses and actions. We both decided to start family meetings because of the number of children we had. Spending time with the children was one of the pastimes we both enjoyed.

Neither of us complained about the number of children nor the lack of friends we had in our early years. We had fun together. We moved to Santa Rosa, California in 1961 from Milwaukee, Wisconsin. There were places we could go to recreate on a tank of gas. We took the children to the Redwood Forest and to the ocean and on picnics. Roy would sing songs while he drove and we all joined in.

The children looked forward to our Monday night family meetings because their Dad would wrestle with them after the meetings were over. During the meetings, which began after supper, everyone sat down and talked. On Mondays, no one could come to visit nor could anyone go outside the house for other activities.

The children also enjoyed family meetings because their father opened up and talked to them, and he answered their questions about relationships, school and anything that was on their minds. This was the time when he became transparent. When the eldest child was 10, he asked for more meetings because he wanted to be near his father. So, Wednesday nights became family meeting night as well.

As I look back on our lives together, without these meetings, our communication would have suffered greatly. Roy began to communicate more easily after years of nonverbal communication or speaking only when he felt it was necessary. His way of speaking was to get directly to the point, but he proved his love through his acts of kindness and caring. His acts left a greater impact than lots of words, and the memories of those times sustain some of the family today.

I continued our family meetings after my husband died at age 38 of an embolism caused by a blood clot that emanated from an Achilles tendon repair, a death that could have been prevented.

When Joshua and I married in 1978 we continued the family meetings. Joshua and I were quite involved in ministries, but on Wednesday evenings and Sunday afternoons we had family meetings. As the children matured and left home, we continued with those who remained. It was such a wonderful way to utilize tools of communication and to help the family interact. I learned to communicate by studying my children's responses and the way each of them opened up at different times.

Spending specific uninterrupted time with one's family not only demonstrates love, it bonds the family and, more importantly, helps to communicate to children that they are important. We found that only a small percentage of communication is speaking. 38 percent is tone of voice, 30 percent body language, and 18 percent action. Only 20 percent involves words.

Joshua wrote a book on family meetings, a tool for communication that we used in our family seminars. Besides the seminars and creative parenting classes, I wrote a column for years called "Ask Ofidean." The issue of communication bears repeating. Communication is to the family as prayer is to the church. Without it, the foundation is unstable. It is the "roto-rooter" in relationships. It unearths and lays the pathway to the heart of the family and to the heart of God.

Over the years and through many experiences we have learned that it takes a variety of techniques to keep communication flowing. At the heart of each method must be the desire to communicate love.

SPEAKING WITHOUT WORDS: Words don't always work for every situation. When I simply wanted to weep and didn't know why, my husband, Joshua, simply held me sometimes weeping with me until I was better. When our children were all home (including the two children we adopted during our marriage) we were also in full-time ministries. We set aside Monday evenings for the two of us and Wednesdays for the children. On Mondays, we closed the living room door from 7-9 p.m. and no one interrupted us. There was an understanding in our house that Mondays were Dad and Mom's night together. We would put on our favorite music and hold hands and quietly listen or hold each other. Sometimes we would even dance slowly around the room just to be close. We seldom spoke the first hour.

TOUCHING HEALS: There are times when a gentle touch will take away the pain. Touching is a wonderful means of communicating. When two people are bonded, a touch is very meaningful. When I sensed any uneasiness in Joshua, I simply placed my hand on his shoulder or on his hand. He did the same with me. We sensed each other's need for a touch. Couples should always practice touching for comfort and affirmation.

LISTENING WITH THE HEART: I listened for what Joshua didn't say, as well as to the words he spoke. It is important to learn to know your spouse well enough to listen to his or her heart. Sometimes I sensed Joshua wanted to please me but really desired to do something else, so I released him. For example, Joshua was a meat and potatoes man. I like salad and gourmet foods. If he knew I didn't want to eat what he wanted to eat, he would take me where I wanted to eat. There are numerous other times when we deferred to each other in more serious decisions concerning travel, the household and the ministry. It is important to learn to listen to the other's heart.

SETTING THE TONE: I did not discuss serious matters when our bedroom needed cleaning because Joshua liked a clean bedroom and scented candles. So I set the tone for discussion. I would also rub his back and his feet when he needed to relax. Since he was my best friend, I sought to please him. Couples should wait until the tone is set for a peaceful discussion of serious matters. Much of the preparation for the verbal communication is non-verbal.

EXPRESSING LOVE: Joshua and I never left the house without speaking of our love for each other. It was not a habit or an afterthought. Think sometimes how you would spend a day without the person you love. This helps remember how much you love them. This love should be expressed daily in words as well as actions.

COMPLIMENTING ONE ANOTHER: Joshua had a habit of asking me if his tie matched the rest of his outfit. I know that if I was not there, he would suit himself up, but he liked me to tell him that he looked good. We wanted to look our best for one another. He complimented me whenever I cooked his favorite dinner or if I wore his favorite dress.

CHECKING RELATIONSHIP: Before we fell asleep at night and before we left our home, one of us would ask, "Is everything well with us?" Joshua usually led the way. If there was anything out of harmony, we would discuss it. On a daily basis, we tried to leave no unsettled issues. That way there was no build-up of disharmony in our marriage.

SHARING THOUGHTS: Joshua was a ponderer. He thought in detail and was deeply concerned about the state of our country. He wept at children being abused, at abortions, senseless killings, etc. He shared these things with me. Admittedly, I did not feel as deeply about some things as he did, but I listened. If he didn't share, he became agitated, which could lead to anger. We prayed about these things and talked about them until a release came.

KEEPING FOCUSED: We did a weekly focus conversation to assure ourselves that we were moving in the plan of God. God has a plan for each family. With all the distractions there are in the world, we needed to keep a consistent focus on what His plan was for us. As we sojourned through this world, we couldn't allow its system to distract us. Some of the questions we asked each other were: "What did you hear from God today?" or "How did your prayer time go?" We compared notes on our conversations with God to be sure we were hearing the same voice. I journaled my conversations and read them occasionally in our quiet time together.

ASSESSING GOALS: What are your expectations? Have they changed in the past two years or six months? Couples need to revisit their expectations of one another especially as they become comfortable in the relationship. This keeps the interest vital. Expectations should be talked about before marriage and on a yearly basis to know whether expectations are being met or whether they can be or should be met.

"There are many things working against the family and especially children. Poverty, divorce, abuse, both physical and mental, are all working for the destruction of the family and against the welfare of children. It takes a lot of effort and love to overcome such destructive elements. Love always wins but, for love to win, it must be communicated."

PEACEFUL TOUCHING: I learned a valuable lesson from a Hispanic sister in one of my Creative Parenting Classes for multicultural parents. I was speaking to them about ways to calm a fretful child and she relayed how she and her husband wash their young children's feet and lotion them slowly while they speak quietly to them. What a wonderful way to serve your children and calm them down at the same time.

Another way to calm a child is to rub their hands gently with lotion. In a market or store, I always hold a child's hand and rub his or her knuckles. Touching gives the child attention, calms them down and communicates love. Remember that this impartation should be done when you are at peace so the child becomes peaceful.

Practice placing your arms around your children whenever you are near them. The closeness is comforting. I pray in my spirit when in the presence of children. It calms them. I do this for my grandchildren on occasion to encourage them to be all that God wants them to be. A little time spent communicating love through touch and prayer is well worth the effort.

COMMUNICATE THE WORD OF GOD EARLY: Instead of placing comic characters in your children's room, place characters from the bible and bible verses above the child's bed. This enables a child to hear the word, which renews their mind, and praying for them in the spirit invites the Holy Spirit.

Part of our ministry for many years was to adoptive parents. We have helped adoptive parents bond with their new arrivals and to think of ways to heal their children's memories. Many children had been in abusive homes, while others were from another culture.

One child I remember vividly was Rahamah. Rahamah's mother, Diane, was a teacher and she followed my advice of putting scripture in Rahamah's room and reading them to her daughter before she left for work each morning. Diane did this consistently from the time Rahamah was adopted. One morning when Rahamah was about nine months old, Diane was late for her part-time teaching job and did not finish reading the scriptures. Rahamah began to whimper as Diane ran out the door. She began to cry loudly when buckled in her car seat. This was unusual because Rahamah loved to ride in the car. Diane checked her hurriedly and decided she needed her diaper changed. When she took her into her room and placed her on the changing table, which was under the scripture that she read each morning, Rahamah began to laugh and pointed. Exasperated, Diane looked up and remembered that she had not completed her morning routine of reading the word of God to Rahamah. Her routine had changed that morning and it bothered Rahamah. After reading the scripture, the child calmed and they left for school.

Diane was surprised. She didn't forget the next day. She was sure that reading the word as she usually did for those nine months really made a difference, but she decided to test whether it was really true. She didn't read the following day and Rahamah began to cry again when they reached the front door.

Another example is the story of a boy named Noel. I gave the parents a tape or Proverbs and asked them to have Noel listen to it before his nap each day. The parents were having a difficult time getting him to sleep without being there. Even as a baby, he had feelings of abandonment. They began playing the tape when he was one month old and, by the time Noel was six months old he wouldn't sleep without Proverbs. He did, however, sleep without the parents in the room when they played the tape.

LISTENING: This is a primary communication tool for any age child especially when they have learned to talk. I spoke of family meetings earlier in this chapter. We used listening times to teach our children godly virtues, which built their character in a godly manner.

These are characteristics we should teach our children in order to prepare them for life outside as well as in the home.

OBEDIENCE is the foundation of a godly person. Children are to obey their parents. A father is responsible to teach this by example as well as the mother, but a father is the enforcer in his home. He obeys his Heavenly Father therefore should expect his children to obey him. He should then insist, out of love and respect for his wife, who is not only his flesh but also his priority, that children obey their mother.

If the father will show forth the love that Christ gave the church (Ephesians 5:25), then regardless of circumstances, he will provide his wife with nurturing and unconditional love so that she will be edified, built up in self-esteem, having a feeling of safety and support from her husband. Women who have this support from their husbands are usually submissive to his leading and this is translated to the children. A husband who does not love and nurture his wife will foster disrespect for womanhood in his sons. The wife who does not show respect and love for her husband will foster this same attitude in her daughters.

COURTESY ALONG WITH KINDNESS AND SHARING are characteristics that can and should be insisted upon in the home, especially between older children. It is difficult at best for adults who have their own ideas of how a house is to be run to live together. Courtesy for each person's feelings and input, kindness toward one another and respect toward the other's privacy and possessions should be emphasized.

PEACE, LIVING HARMONIOUSLY TOGETHER, should be taught by showing children how to deal with anger. When our children were growing up, they were not allowed to strike one another to settle an argument or disagreement. If they were angry, we would allow them to tell each other how they felt, within boundaries. Some psychologists may not agree, but I believe anger should be vented and not kept inside to fester and turn to hatred and resentment. I recommend that children be allowed to vent as long as it's done without calling names or hitting. Children should not be allowed to shove, hit curse or yell. They should also be given a time limit to say what they want to say. This way they can speak out their anger and be listened to. Each child should have an opportunity to speak without being interrupted.

Another way to vent is to use a nerf ball to throw outside at a tree. Some children cannot express how they feel until they are calm. Other ways can be found to encourage peaceable ways to settle a disagreement and one important one is for parents to encourage each child to speak while the other listens attentively. When each child has finished (give them a time limit), offer a solution that they can understand. If the children are old enough, ask them to offer a solution for their problem.

WORK IS A VITAL ASPECT OF A HAPPY LIFE and should be taught to children in their early years. Give children chores as early as possible. Teach them to pick up their own toys and place them in a designated place. Teach both boys and girls to make their own beds, showing them how and praising them as they learn.

I began teaching chores at 18 months, by showing my eldest son how to pick up his toys and clapping delightedly when he put even one away. I hugged him and told him I appreciated him. Young children like to please their parents. He had his first job pulling weeds and mowing lawns by age 8. By age 12, he purchased his own lawn mower and tools with the money he saved.

ORDERLINESS SHOULD BE TAUGHT TO CHILDREN through regular habits and a well-ordered life. Meals in the family should not be so sporadic that children eat junk food to appease themselves. Bedtime should he regulated and consistent. Children should be encouraged to read quietly or read to the family, or listen to soft worship music before bedtime. When children are small lotion them down with warm olive oil or baby oil after a bath and tell them how much you love them.

FINANCES SHOULD BE TAUGHT TO CHILDREN. We taught our children early, between ages 3 and 6 years to give 10 percent of their income to God, 10 percent in the piggy bank and the rest of their earned money could be used for themselves. They earned money from the age of 8, not for cleaning their rooms because that's part of what families do as good stewards. They earned for helping someone else, like the neighbor, picking up papers off their yard or raking leaves.

RESPECTING THEMSELVES AND OTHERS is also something that children should be taught. We didn't allow our children to yell at us, and we didn't yell at them nor were they allowed to yell at each other or to take things from each other without asking first.

Parents should question themselves to check whether they are building good character traits in their children. Engage children in communication. If you have a non-verbal child, this child needs an atmosphere created for him/her to open up and communicate. This depends on the parents. Non-verbal parents are the child's models. Since the primary influence of parents on the behavior of their child is from birth to 8 years of age, then whatever behavior you want the child to exemplify should be learned during this crucial trainable period. If you "aren't there yet," encourage your child to speak by making an audiotape for your child to listen to. Sometimes it's easier for non-verbal parents to talk to their child when they are not face-to-face. This can be fun too. Speak into the tape, pause and allow the child to talk.

Of course, this is only one way to involve a child in conversation and listening. The best way is to personally keep talking and listening to the child. Talking to your child helps you to begin to verbalize more, which helps both you and the child. After a time of consistency, the child will begin to respond.

SOME TOPICS OF CONVERSATION:

Express feelings by talking about how you feel. Choose good positive feelings to begin with to encourage the child to express his or her feelings.

- Talk about the seasons, the weather, birds, anything that will expose the child to the outside world.

- Read to the child and ask questions.

- Ask about school.

- Ask the child what he or she likes and dislikes.

- Children respond to the closeness of a parent, so hug and hold our child while you are talking.

OTHER WAYS OF REARING GODLY CHILDREN—A single parent wrote me when I was writing a column for the local newspaper called "Ask Ofidean." She wrote "I am about to go crazy. I am a single parent rearing two teenagers, a boy and a girl. My girl is 13 and wants to date already. She hangs around with kids who are involved in smoking marijuana and likes to hang out on street corners. My son is 15 and he tries very hard to be helpful around the house. He has a part-time job, and now he has friends who tell him he should have more fun. I've noticed that he's staying out later and later. I work eight 8 to 10 hours a day and can't find the time I need to spend with them. It's so frustrating. Sometimes I work on Saturdays to earn extra money to make ends meet. My ex-husband is in prison and I receive no child support."

If you are a single parent experiencing communication problems like this parent who wrote me, let me give general advice to singles who are raising children alone. You should begin preparing your children for life with one parent when they are ages 1 through 5. Don't wait until they are teenagers to begin preparing them. Teach them to face a world which is full of frustration and chaos.

First, establish your priorities. You and your children are Number 1. Do not try to keep up with other families. Arrange your schedule to fit their personal needs. Single parents cannot work all day, spend their evenings away from their children and then on weekends leave their children alone. You must sacrifice some of your free time in the early years in order to establish a strong value system in your children. Your children are victims not perpetrators. They did not ask to be in a single parent home. If you provide a stable home life early, they will be able to make right choices when they are older.

TEEN-AGERS:
- Spend some time with your children before work. Get up a half-hour earlier than usual to begin the day smoothly. Children should begin their day positively. Take time to

talk to them at the breakfast table. It's worth the half-hour of lost sleep to build up your children.

- Pray with your children at any age. Hold them close and tell them how much you love them. Even when they are young adults, if you repeat it over and over, and accompany it with affection, this action will be a source of comfort.

- Do not allow your children to constantly watch television. If you do allow them to watch television, spend time with them FIRST. They deserve some of your undivided attention.

- Manage your money well enough to give your children a proper breakfast. Pre-sweetened cereals are not nutritious enough. It's better to give them toast and juice.

- Before leaving for work, talk to your teens about your expectations and what you need from them. Take time out during the week to have meetings with them. Have them help you with your schedule.

- Plan outings with your teenagers. It's worth a YMCA or Salvation Army membership to take them swimming. Take your daughter with you to exercise class. Include your children in your life. Once a month spend a Saturday with your daughter or son window-shopping, go walking together, take a class together, or attend a parenting seminar. There are many things you can do together.

- Get help with your budget management and cut back on your work hours, if you can. Measure the time you spend with your children against the time they spend with others who talk to them. Their actions are a response to the consistency of relationships and what they absorb. Children left to their own devices make decisions based on who and what they value most. The parent still has the greatest influence on their children if they take the time.

SINGLE PARENTS OF YOUNG CHILDREN:

- Form a single parent co-op. Take time to search out a good child-care program if you are parenting young children.

- Call your children on your lunch break and tell them that you love them and you are looking forward to seeing them when you return home. A young child needs to hear his or her mother's voice during the long work/travel period.

- Do not send your children to bed without spending at least an hour with them. When you pick up your children from day care, take them with you to do errands. Talk to them, even though you may be tired. Tell them you are tired but you want to be with them.

- Your children come first before telephoning friends. It's so important to manage your time to meet your children's needs so that you may meet your own needs without guilt or frustration. Begin early having family meetings with your children.

- Talk to them at the dinner table. Do not allow your children to spend their important mealtime with someone else. Children must learn that family time is important. This gives you a chance to discuss their day and teach them your values. This time is also important for winding down, touching and bonding, listening to their needs and providing them with the individual attention they need to feel loved and wanted.

- Before retiring, if you must watch television, watch it with your children.

- Always hug them before putting them to bed. This gives you the rest of the evening after they are sound asleep to spend on yourself.

I am frequently asked how I managed studying for a doctorate while raising eight children. I believe that each person is unique and born for a purpose. I had to find out what my purpose was. Although there were others in my early years that I wished to emulate, I could only be myself and I learned to love myself and concentrate on my life goals.

I achieved my goals by establishing priorities at the appropriate times. I used good management of the time I had to accomplish each task. My priorities were God, my husband, my children and my career. My career and ministry to families were carried out simultaneously. In order for me to succeed in my career/ministry, I first had to learn what my goals, gifts and abilities were, and how to maximize the time that I had to do all that I desired to do.

I learned early before marriage that "To everything there is a season and a time for every purpose under the heaven." (Ecclesiastes 3:1) There is a balance to living and anything done out of season will not succeed. Some of my goals were:

• Complete college and earn a graduate degree. Since I had no financial support from parents, that meant I had to work harder, so I began to work outside the home at 12 and continued that pattern through high school and college.

• I wanted to get married and have a large family.

I married after 2-1/2 years of college. I returned to school after my eighth child was born, taking one class per semester to begin with so that it would not interfere with my family's needs. During this time, I trained my children to care for each other. I volunteered in their schools in order to keep abreast of each child's education. I also volunteered in the community to provide them with the extra-curricular enrichment they needed.

I maintained a schedule for house duties and set aside time for my husband and children. During the kids' naptimes and at bedtime, when my husband was not home I studied. Later, as I completed my graduate studies, I took all the children to the library with me. They learned to love those outings.

My full-time career began after my eighth child was in pre-school. I taught at the university where I received my master's degree and simultaneously directed a statewide program for students. My husband and I synchronized our schedules so that one of us would be home while the other was away. I did not mix the seasons of my achievements. They flowed together in balance. I also desired to travel, which I have done. I traveled extensively in other countries as well as the United States. This is now my season of imparting wisdom that I have learned to inspire others.

There is a tendency for me to overdo because I am a creative person. So at this point in my life, it's time to slow down the pace and establish appropriate priorities again. I believe that any time you spend with your children when you can listen and just be there is "quality." Make every minute count. Each thing you do with your children is good when your motivation is one of sharing yourself.

There are some ideas for the busy mother that helped me in my early years of parenting. My children learned to enjoy the things I enjoyed doing, which gave them time with me and also provided me with the pleasure I needed, especially since I reared eight biological children who, except for two, are less than two years apart. Joshua and I later adopted two more girls.

I did not work outside of the home on a consistent basis until my youngest child was in preschool. But I did work in between pregnancies to help financially. I also took college courses in between births and completed four degrees after giving birth to eight children.

I loved to read but seldom found the time to myself. So twice weekly, after dinner, I took all eight of my children to the library with me. Before I began their outings, my husband and I taught the children to be responsible to each other by pairing them off. The eldest took the youngest, the second eldest watched the seventh child, and the third child took the sixth child and the fourth and fifth stayed with me. We taught them stories to tell each other on the way to the library. Once at the library, the children went to the children's section and the youngest of the children listened to cassette tapes of children's music and stories. The oldest children did their homework and read books, and the middle children learned to use the card catalog. Each child had their turn helping me study in twos because this privilege afforded them special time. The ones who could not read the card catalogs and underline my magazine articles held my book while I read or they would look at pictures in magazines. When they were cooperative for one hour, which allowed me enough time to check references and read 15-20 pages of material, they were rewarded with 15 minutes of special time with me after everyone returned home.

During this time, I would read them a story that they selected. This way they could stay up 15 minutes later, which was indeed a prize. I never rewarded good behavior with candy or money. These only temporarily affect behavior and leave a false expectation for doing well. Appreciation by complimentary remarks, hugs and "I love you's" are very effective in parenting children.

Both my husband, Roy and I enjoyed music and theater. In order for us to have our music time together, we had to teach the children to enjoy those things too. During those early childrearing years, we couldn't afford to go out much so we made our own music-theater workshop in our living room. We assessed our children's abilities early. Some were natural comedians, others could read well, others wrote short stories, all loved to sing. My husband and I were the audience, which gave us an opportunity to hold hands, eat popcorn and reminisce about our dating days.

Another time the children looked forward to was our "special outing" once a month. With each monthly paycheck we saved

$10.00 which doesn't go far these days. But in the 1960's, we could put $2.00 of regular gasoline in "Betsy," our green station wagon, and go to the hot dog stand. Each child would get a hotdog and milk for .75 cents. Afterward, we would spend time at the park where the children would play on the slides, swings, monkey bars, etc. My husband and I would walk and talk together. Since we lived in Northern California, every other month we budgeted an extra $2.00 for gas and took the children to the Redwoods, Petrified Forest and the Russian River. My husband and I enjoyed these outings as much as the children did.

Rearing your children can be a joyful time as long as you begin early and determine how you want your family life to be. God, who created all good things, ordains time spent creatively. Be wise and gear your precious time around activities in which all can participate and develop good communication skills. This way the family can always enjoy each other, even after they have grown up because your interests are similar.

There are basic effective elements of communication that connect the marriage and family into healthy relational units and bring harmony to a family.

A basic element of effective communication is the integrity of the spoken word and a sensitive listening ear. A listening ear indicates the desire to understand and accept what is being said.

An excellent example of receiving communication is that of Jeremiah, Ezekiel and the Apostle John who ate the word of God. Each made the word of God a part of himself. When a spouse is speaking, it is important that the other partner gives his or her entire attention, which involves the whole body.

In the marriage relationship the need to hear and act is important to changing negative situations in a marriage. Good communication requires commitment, hard work and respect for the other person's opinion. Some of the major hindrances to effective communication are:

1. Lack of interest, the heart is not open to receive.

2. Assumptions based on feelings and not fact.

3. Hiding iniquity in our hearts.

4. Lack of patience.

5. Fear

On every level, communication should become the primary key to marriage and family relationships. Communication brings about knowledge and understanding of your spouse, which is why the scripture emphasizes communication. This knowledge and understanding is key to imparting good communication skills to children.

Before marriage, couples should communicate their expectations and establish their goals. This process should continue throughout the marriage. Reviewing expectations periodically is a tool for communication, which contributes to marital growth. A couple's relationship will continually grow, if they are motivated toward keeping each other informed of their changing expectation and goals.

Before establishing goals for marriage, decide whether they are realistic. These goals should be spoken to your partner. Many times goals are never fulfilled in a marriage because they have not been spoken only expected. Bringing them into the open is necessary. Remember every person who marries goes into the marriage with certain expectations. The trouble begins when the expectations aren't met. Unfortunately, the other person doesn't know what these expectations are if they are not spoken. This is why honest communication before and throughout marriage is important. How many times have you heard a husband or wife say that the other spouse should already know how or what to do." Each one thinks that understanding should be automatic. Oftentimes men do not know how to nurture a woman's emotions because they haven't been taught and haven't seen it demonstrated. A woman doesn't always understand how to treat her husband's silences or his priorities in their relationship. She has to learn.

Communication is such a key ingredient in healthy relationship both in the marriage and with family members.

Reflections

What are your expectations for a happy marriage relationship?

_____

_____

_____

_____

_____

When and how do you communicate best?

_____

_____

_____

_____

_____

Do you understand the communication components--tone, words, body language, from the heart? How will you use them?

_____

_____

_____

_____

_____

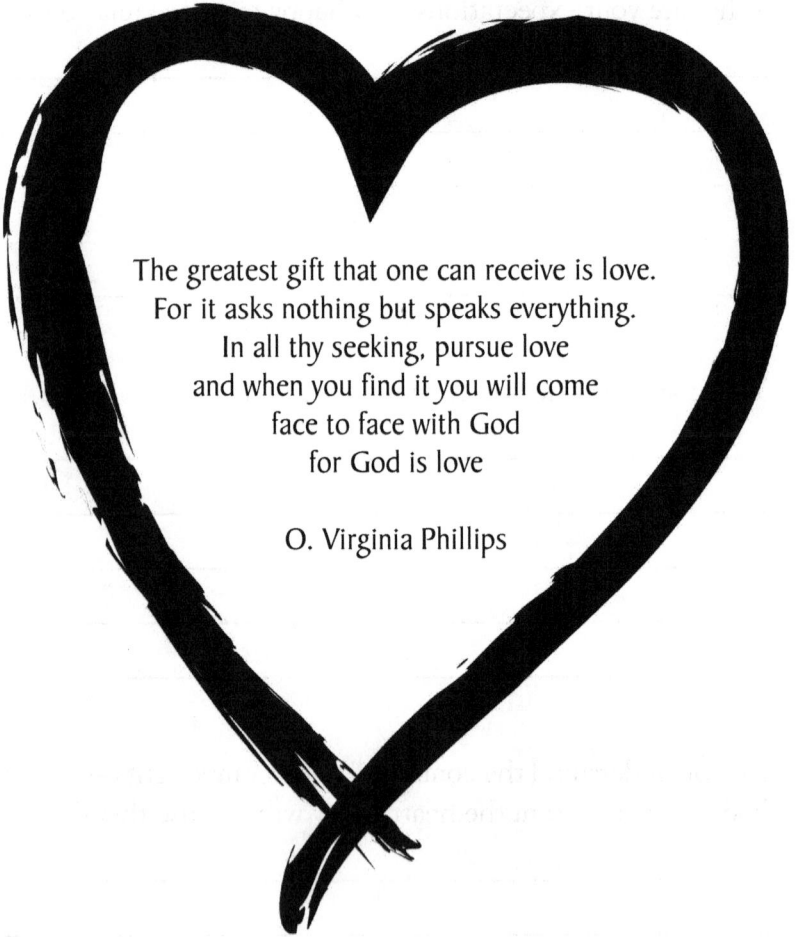

The greatest gift that one can receive is love.
For it asks nothing but speaks everything.
In all thy seeking, pursue love
and when you find it you will come
face to face with God
for God is love

O. Virginia Phillips

7

THE LOVE CONNECTION

ENDURANCE

During the years that I was widowed, I kept my children in church. We lived in a small town in Oregon called Sherwood, which is approximately 17 miles south of Portland, Oregon. We attended Maranatha church in Portland at least four times a week because I was involved in so much there.

I became good friends with the pastor and his wife, John and Yvonne Garlington. In fact, my eight children and I were one of the first families to invite them to our home when they arrived in Portland to pastor in 1977. I had attended the church for one year before they came. Yvonne and I became good friends and our children spent a lot of time together. Our home was always filled with youth and many young people received Christ at our home.

When Yvonne's mother died, I accompanied her to her mother's home going in Cleveland, Ohio. She felt that, as a widow, I would know how to comfort her father. I went gladly and even read the obituary at the service, although I was not related biologically. Yvonne's father, Joshua, and I became good friends. I believe we knew soon afterwards that God had intended us to meet and marry.

We married in August 1978. We had to overcome many obstacles, one of which was miraculously resolved and that was whether Joshua could love again after 32 years of marriage to Ruby, his first wife. His grief was short lived. He hurt so badly that he begged God for relief. One morning, he awakened and looked at his wife's photograph, and it felt as though she had been gone for years instead of months. God took all his grief and gave Joshua an unfeigned love for me that was so unconditional it wrapped itself around my children, and he became their father.

He adopted all eight of my children when we married and stepparent was never mentioned in our household. He was Dad from the very beginning. Joshua even suggested that the children use Mitchell-Phillips, so that they would honor the name of their birth father. As we discussed our deceased spouses, we discovered that each of us shared some of the same characteristics. For example, his wife Ruby was an educator and had a prophetic ministry and so do I. Roy, my former spouse, served in the Marine Corp, as had Joshua. They both had the same rank and they both enjoyed cooking. Both were philosophers and deep thinking men who pondered about almost everything.

One great difference was that Joshua was a communicator, something I longed for, and Roy was not. Joshua and I began our relationship by praying a lot and listening for God's instructions. When God promised us a perfect marriage Joshua didn't believe it. Neither of us had ever seen a perfect marriage and we didn't know what one looked like. But, being a dreamer, I wanted a perfect marriage so I believed it was possible.

We initially thought a perfect marriage was one without conflict. But we learned that conflict helps strengthen a marriage if conflicts are resolved unselfishly. God revealed to us that a marriage relationship is perfect when it is mature through the love of Jesus Christ. If we would seek to know the heart of God. He promised that, as our head, He would teach us how to have a perfect marriage. But we needed to obey the principles provided in this book.

Each principle was worked out in our marriage relationship. The same principles are accomplished in the body of Christ, the church, when applied. Our confidence was in the Creator of the marriage relationship. Marriage was wondrous, joyous, and peaceful for us because we saw it as God meant it to be. That doesn't mean we totally overcame conflict, but we took our conflicts to Jesus. He is love, and love is the key to a perfect marriage.

Our marriage was a **no-fault** marriage. Joshua believed that whatever happened in our marriage, he was responsible. If there was conflict he looked for something he did or didn't do. Because I was his best friend and I honored his position as the head of the household, he blamed me for nothing.

This is difficult for some couples to believe, but Joshua explained it this way:

A father is not to blame for everything that happens within his household, but he is responsible. For example, in a corporation, if something goes wrong, the head of the corporation is ultimately responsible for what goes on in his or her establishment because he or she is the leader.

As a **Prophet** in the home, God wants to give a husband foresight concerning his family. God not only forewarns, but has also offers encouragement to the husband. As King, God has given the husband power to rule with love and kindness. If he does not rule with love and kindness, the becomes a dictator. He is not only responsible for the care of his family, food, clothing and shelter, but he is also responsible for spiritual food and covering.

The husband also becomes a facilitator and delegator in his home. As the **Priest**, he goes before the Lord on behalf of his family and seeks direction because he is the spiritual leader. This does not mean that the wife and children do not seek the Lord for themselves; it does not take away their individuality before God. The husband is responsible for spiritual leadership in his home. Just as Jesus intercedes before the Father for us, the husband intercedes for his family. Jesus is the responsible head of the church and the husband is the responsible head of his wife.

In the home where the father does not take these responsibilities, it becomes difficult for the wife. If she takes the responsibilities that God has intended the husband and father to have, the pressures can become too great unless God intervenes. He does, for those women who seek after Him to do His will. He will intervene in a home where there is a widow or a single parent. Jesus will Himself become the covering.

So the authority God has given the husband and father, if used according to God's word, will be upheld and backed by Jesus. The husband and father can bring about changes in moods and attitudes in his home by exercising love, prayer and the authority of the word. God will honor the role of leadership that He has given that husband and father.

Wives should pray for their husbands. And, in their daily devotion, pray that God will continue to give him the wisdom, knowledge and strength to be the spiritual leader of the home. There is then no feeling in that husband or father of superiority, if he understands his role. It does not place the wife in a subservient position at all because they are one flesh. Neither does she lose her spiritual identity because whoever is born of the Spirit becomes as the Son of God. Here, women become "sons" as the man in the church becomes the "bride," for in the Lord there is neither male nor female. This is not to be confused with God's intention for male and female in the flesh, because these roles are clearly defined in scripture.

As man gives himself complete submission to the Lord, this brings about the submission of the wife. This is not strange because the word of God tells us in (James 1:22),

"But be ye doers of the word, and not hearers only...".

The father should be an example of what he learns and teaches. A father can decide what kind of harvest he wants by what he sows. For he will reap the fruit of his doing whether it be good or bad.

The wife's role in the home is that of a virtuous woman who is to be trusted. She does good to her husband and family all the days of her life (Proverbs 31). Virtue and ability are not to be confused. If a woman has abilities to sell, write, sew or whatever she is gifted to and her husband loves her, he will free her to pursue those things. It will benefit her and the family and seek to bring joy to her heart.

A virtuous woman will not allow her career to interfere with the welfare of her family. She can be trusted. She will build her home, not tear it down. This will require the agreement of both the husband and wife. When both of them agree before God, He is in the midst of them, guiding them both. A mother can influence what happens in her home when she loves God and her family. In Proverbs 1:8, the scripture tells the children to "hear the instruction of thy father and forsake not the law of thy mother." Both father and mother are responsible for the training and instruction of their children.

Many of today's mothers must juggle home and work, so how are children included in a mature marriage? There are ways to purposely plan a happy family. It happens with applying godly principles and right timing so you can achieve your goals by setting priorities. This does not mean that children will grow up into perfect adults but they must be prepared to face life with godly principles.

Mothers who are home most of the day can take time to train up a child and the father can reaffirm what the mother teaches. He can teach his children to obey their mother by the support he gives to her.

God's blueprint for a successful marriage is that husbands dwell with their wives according to knowledge, assigning them honor as the weaker vessel (the rib section is easily bruised or broken). (1 Peter 3:7) This means being considerate of her opinion, likes and dislikes, and not belittling her or embarrassing her but learning to know her and being sensitive to her emotional needs. The woman is usually more sensitive emotionally than a man. That's what is meant by "the weaker vessel."

When the husband works hard at being the proper leader it is not burdensome for the wife to be submissive in all things. God gave the authority to the husband to lead. Inherent in this are the offices of prophet, king and priest because he is set aside to serve the Lord and represents Jesus in directing his family.

"When the perfect comes, the partial will be done away" (1 Corinthians 13:10).

Love is the perfect partner in marriage. Learning to love is developing a continuing relationship with Jesus and your spouse. Below is a marriage modeled after 1 Corinthians 13:4-8.

Motivation   Commitment does not seek its own.

Acceptance   Unconditional, believes all things.

Restraint   Patient, is not provoked, does not act unbecoming.

Resilient   Bears all things.

Involvement   Endures all things.

Acquiescence   Does not take into account a wrong suffered, does not rejoice in unrighteousness, but rejoices with the truth and forgives.

Giving   Does not brag, is not arrogant, sows good seed.

Eternal   Never Fails.

THREE TYPES OF LOVE
FOR A SUCCESSFUL MARRIAGE

EROS This kind of love seeks sensual expression. Eros is a romantic love, sexual love. It is inspired by the biological structure of human nature. The husband and wife, in a good marriage, will love each other romantically and emotionally.

PHILIA This type of love is good in a marriage. The husband and wife are best friends. This friendship means companionship, communication and cooperation.

AGAPE This is an unconditional giving, gifting love. The kind of love that goes on loving even when the other becomes unlovable. AGAPE is not just something that happens to you. It is something that happens in you. This love is a personal act of commitment. Agape is Christ's love.

Christ's love is kindness. It is being sympathetic, thoughtful and sensitive to the needs of your loved ones.

Christ's love is contentment and forgiving love.

Christ's love is a Heart Connection.

Christ's love for us is sacrificial love.

Christ's love is unconditional.

Christ's love is an eternal love.

If individuals will put forth effort purposely to increase PHILIA and AGAPE love, the EROS love will be enriched so that it becomes less demanding. Love in marriage and the family involves a heart connection to the heart of God and brings about the knowledge and understanding needed to belong, to be one, to have friendship, commitment, submission and communication which are the fruit of healthy relationships.

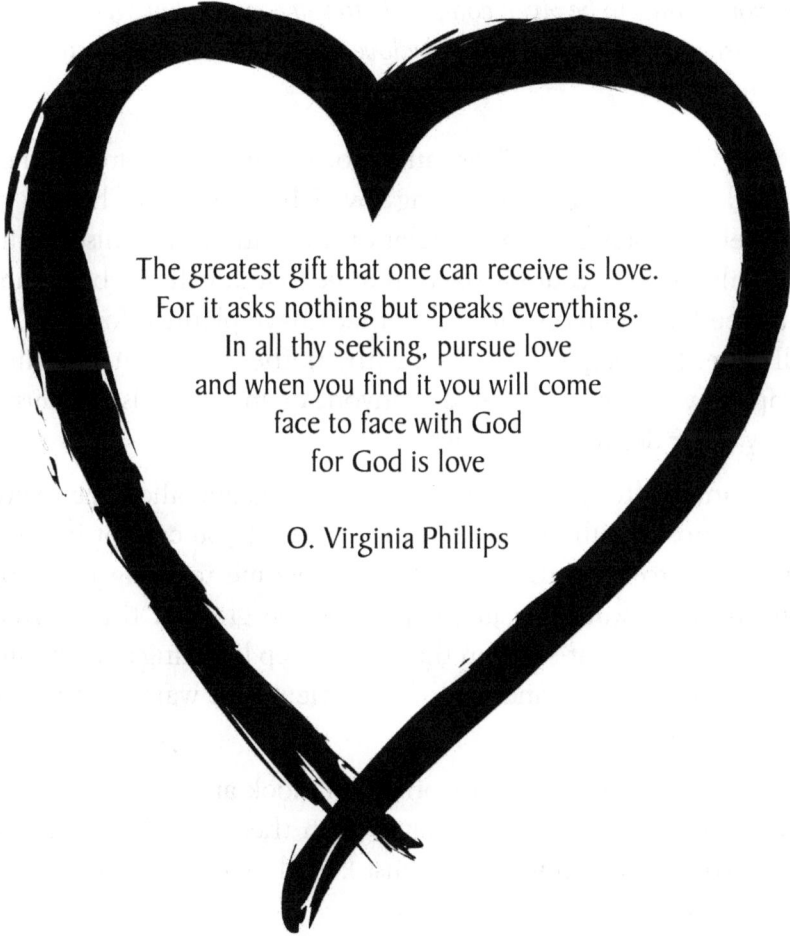

The greatest gift that one can receive is love.
For it asks nothing but speaks everything.
In all thy seeking, pursue love
and when you find it you will come
face to face with God
for God is love

O. Virginia Phillips

LOVE

Everyone wants to be given completely to someone, to have a deep, good relationship with another; and to be loved thoroughly and exclusively.

But God says to a Christian, "No, not until you are satisfied, fulfilled and content with being loved by Me alone; having an intensely personal and unique relationship with me and discovering that only in me is your satisfaction to be found, will you be capable of the perfect human relationship that I have planned for you. You will never he completely united with another until you are united completely with me; exclusive of anyone or anything else; exclusive of any other desires or longings.

I want you to stop planning, stop wishing, and allow me to give you the most thrilling plan existing, one that you cannot imagine. I want you to have the best. Please allow me to bring it to you. You just keep watching me, expecting the greatest things. Keep experiencing the satisfaction that I am. Keep listening and learning the things I promise and mean. Be patient and wait for my Holy Spirit to direct you.

Don't be anxious. Don't worry, don't look around at the things others have gotten or that I have given them. Don't look at the things you think you want. You just keep looking up to me or you will miss what I want to show you.

And then, when you are ready, I'll surprise you with a love far more wonderful than any you would dream of. I am working even at this moment to have both you ready at the same time and until you are ready, and until the one I have for you is ready, until you are both satisfied with me and the life I want you to have, you will not be able to experience the love that exemplifies your relationship with me, a perfect love.

And dear one, I want you to have this most wonderful love. I want you to see in the flesh a picture of your relationship with me, and to enjoy perfection and love that only I offer. Know that I love you completely. I am God Almighty, believe me and be satisfied."

O. Virginia Phillips

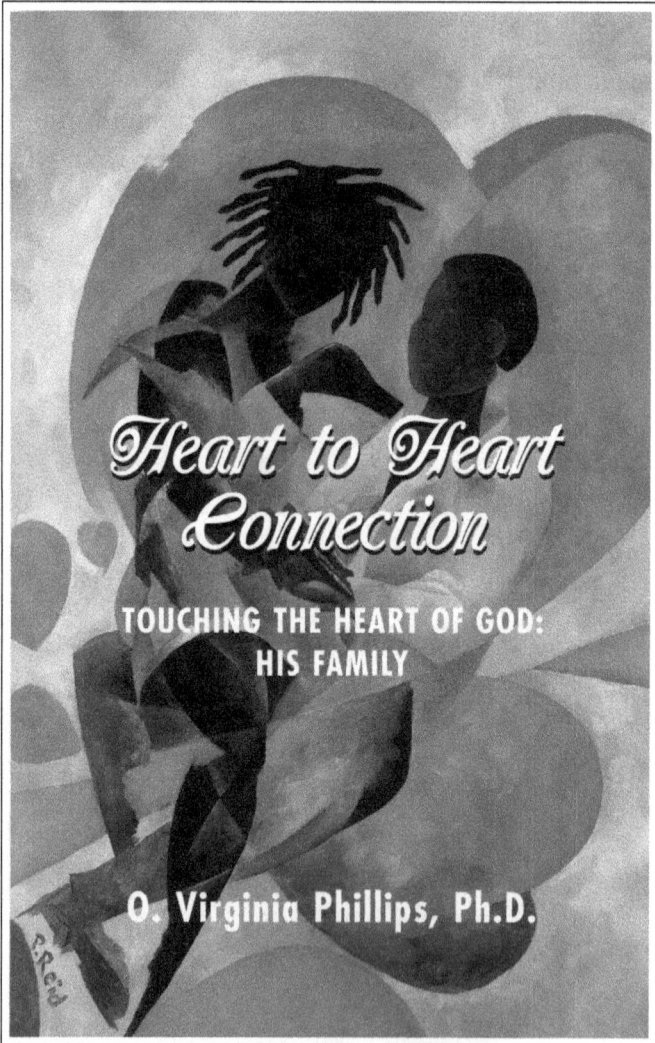

Heart to Heart Connection

TOUCHING THE HEART OF GOD:
HIS FAMILY

O. Virginia Phillips, Ph.D.

First Printing bookcover design
by Philemon Reid
July 1, 1945 - June 9, 2009

ABOUT THE AUTHOR

Dr. O. V. Phillips, a pioneer in intervention programs for preservation and permanency in families, is also an inspirational lecturer and author, writing columns for several newspapers. For many years she has written children's stories to leave a legacy for her grandchildren. In 1994 Dr. Phillips authored the book *Ashes to Life*. She has taught marriage and educational seminars, family meetings, churches and conferences including: National Women's Aglow, U.S. Department of Education, Consortium for Northern California Child Development Centers, African American Cultural Exchange Program, University Without Walls in San Francisco, OMSI and places all around the United States and internationally, including East, West and North Africa, Haiti and the British West Indies.

She is co-founder of *Give Us This Day, Inc.*, Family Ministries Director of *One Church, One Child of Oregon*, President and Founder of *Women of Purpose, International*, a family ministry whose purpose is to build relationships and bring unity through Reconciliation, Restoration, and Renewal across denominational, social, ethnic and cultural groups.

ABOUT THE PREVIOUS COVER ARTIST

Philemon Reid was a well-known, acclaimed Northwest artist whose technique is a form of cubism. Over the last several years his subject matter had been musical in content. His painting technique is to mix the paint on canvas as he paints.

To purchase additional copies of this book
by Dr. O. Virginia Phillips,
or copies of her other books:

On-line purchasing:
www.womenofpurpose.com
Click on the BOOKSTORE tab
... or find it at
createspace.com/5649770
... or, Amazon.com

If you prefer not to order on-line:

Women of Purpose, International office
Call: 503-443-2007 (Oregon)
(Tues-Thurs., 10am - 3pm)

or Email
info@womenofpurpose.com

www.ingramcontent.com/pod-product-compliance
Lightning Source LLC
Chambersburg PA
CBHW052113090426
42741CB00009B/1796